ULTIMATE SOUPS

For Healthy Living

JENNY STACEY

Published in 2001 by Caxton Editions
20 Bloomsbury Street
London WC1B 3JH
a member of the Caxton Publishing Group

© 2001 Caxton Publishing Group

Designed and produced for Caxton Editions
by Open Door Limited
Langham, Rutland
Editing: Alison Leach
Typesetting: Jane and Richard Booth
Colour separation: GA Graphics, Stamford

Title: Ultimate Soups
ISBN: 1 84067 353 2

Printed and bound by CTPS

ULTIMATE SOUPS

For Healthy Living

JENNY STACEY

CAXTON EDITIONS

CONTENTS

Making your own soup from fresh ingredients is extremely rewarding and enjoyable, and you will certainly appreciate the contrast to commercially produced soups when you taste the end results. There is nothing quite like a home-made soup for flavour, texture and colour. Warming and nutritious, home-made soups are simple to prepare and are easily stored for ease of use either in the refrigerator or freezer. Ideal as a starter on a cold winter's day or as a light lunch or supper, soups come in many different guises and incorporate many different ingredients. Some are meals in themselves, being thick and hearty with rice, pasta or pulses added, while others are light and should be served as a preface to a meal. Chilled soups are now very popular and are ideal on a hot summer's day for a picnic or as an elegant starter for a summer's evening garden supper. Grimod de La Reynière once wrote, 'Soup is to dinner what the porch or gateway is to a building', which is very true.

The word soup has developed from 'sop', a term originally applied to bread dipped in water or wine before being eaten. Broth was the liquid in which meat had been boiled with additional flavourings and pottage a thick version of the broth to which chopped meats were added. Today the term soup is applied to a more sophisticated version of broth, and comes in many forms.

When planning a meal with a soup as a starter, it is important to consider the courses to follow in terms of ingredients and 'weight' in order to give a good balance.

Soups are basically thick or thin. One of the most important considerations when making a soup is the base liquid, which can be simply water if the soup ingredients are going to give a good flavour, such as spinach, asparagus or pulses, or it can be one of four basic stocks: beef, chicken, fish or vegetable. These stocks give an excellent basic flavour to consommés, creamy soups, thick or puréed soups and clear broths. A quick and easy recipe for a tomato base is also given, which is ideal for pasta sauces, too.

The stocks are quite simple to prepare and, if prepared in larger batches, may be frozen in suitable quantities or as ice cubes, so that a tasty soup can be made in minutes, or the stocks may be used as an excellent base for sauces.

The following recipes give basic ingredients, but you may add others as liked, such as washed vegetable peelings and beef or chicken bones to concentrate the flavour of the stock.

When cooking stock, be sure to bring it to the boil slowly to ensure a clear result. Fast boiling will result in a murky stock. For meat and poultry stocks, only use raw bones for a really clear result. Keep the ingredients in large pieces for clear stocks and remove scum from the surface constantly to clear the liquid.

BEEF STOCK

Makes 2.5 litres/4¹/₂ pints/2³/₄ quarts

3 tablespoons oil
1.5 kg/3¹/₄ lb beef bones
350 g/12 oz shin of beef
3 litres/5¹/₄ pints/3¹/₂ quarts cold water
2 celery sticks, chopped
2–3 carrots, roughly chopped
2 brown onions, roughly chopped with skin on
2 tomatoes, halved
few sprigs of thyme
1 bay leaf

Heat 2 tablespoons of the oil in a large pan and brown the bones and shin of beef until well coloured. (Or put them in a large roasting pan in a pre-heated oven at 220°C/425°F/Gas 7.) Pour off any fat and add the water to the pan. Bring to the boil slowly.

Skim off any scum from the top of the stock, reduce the heat and simmer for 2 hours, skimming the top as required.

Heat the remaining oil in a large frying pan and cook the chopped vegetables until browned, turning frequently. Add to the beef stock with the tomatoes, thyme and bay leaf. Simmer, uncovered, for another 1 hour.

Strain the stock through a sieve lined with paper towels or muslin cheesecloth. As the stock cools, any fat will rise to the top. To remove this fat while the stock is warm, drag a paper towel across the top of the stock. Alternatively, allow the stock to cool and lift off the layer of fat that sets on the top.

CHICKEN STOCK

Makes 2 litres/3¹/₂ pints/2¹/₄ quarts

1.75 kg/3¹/₃ lb–2 kg/4¹/₂ lb chicken carcass
 or chicken pieces
2.5 litres/4¹/₂ pints/2³/₄ quarts cold water
6 black peppercorns
12 parsley sprigs
few sprigs of thyme (optional)
2 white onions, roughly chopped with skin on
2 celery sticks, chopped
2 carrots, chopped

Put the chicken in a large pan with the remaining ingredients and slowly bring to the boil.

Skim the top of the soup and reduce the heat to a simmer. Simmer gently, uncovered, for 3 hours. Strain the stock and remove the fat.

FISH STOCK

Makes 750 ml/1¹/₄ pints/3 cups

500 g/18 oz fish bones, heads and trimmings, washed
900 ml/3 pints/1 quart cold water
1 onion, roughly chopped
1 celery stick, roughly chopped
6 white peppercorns
1 mace blade or large pinch of ground nutmeg
1 teaspoon salt

Put the fish pieces and water in a large pan and bring to the boil. Skim off any discoloured froth from the top and add the remaining ingredients to the pan.

Cook, uncovered, for 30 minutes. Do not overcook, otherwise the stock will be bitter. Strain the stock and discard the bones and vegetables. Use within 2 days of making or freeze for later use.

VEGETABLE STOCK

10 medium-sized carrots
5 medium-sized onions
half a head of celery, including leaves
15 g/^{1}/$_2$ oz/1 tablespoon butter
4 black peppercorns
1 teaspoon tomato purée (paste)
mixed vegetable scraps

Roughly chop all the vegetables. Melt the butter in a large saucepan and brown the vegetables, turning frequently.

Add all the remaining ingredients and cover with cold water. Bring to the boil slowly, then reduce the heat, cover and simmer for 2 hours.

Strain the liquid and discard the vegetables and seasonings. Store in the refrigerator for 2–3 days or freeze for later use.

WHITE STOCK

1.5 kg/3¹/₄ lb veal bones
2 onions, quartered
2 medium-sized carrots
1 celery stick, chopped
1 bouquet garni
6 black peppercorns
2 teaspoons salt

Place the bones in a large saucepan or stock pot and two-thirds cover with cold water. Bring to the boil slowly, skimming the surface constantly.

Add the remaining ingredients to the pan, then reduce the heat and simmer, uncovered, for 4 hours.

Strain the stock, allow to cool and remove the fat from the surface.

TOMATO BASE

2 x 400 g/14 oz cans plum tomatoes
3 tablespoons olive oil
1 teaspoon caster (super fine) sugar
¹/₂ teaspoon salt
¹/₂ teaspoon freshly ground black pepper
24 fresh basil leaves

Chop the tomatoes finely and place in a saucepan with the juices from the cans. Add all the remaining ingredients except the basil, stir well and cook over a medium heat for 10 minutes.

Tear the basil leaves and add to the mixture. Cook for another 10 minutes and allow to cool for storage or use as required.

STORAGE OF STOCKS

Once prepared and completely cooled, these stocks may be stored, covered in the refrigerator for 2–3 days or frozen in rigid containers in suitable quantities. Alternatively, freeze in ice-cube trays and use as bases for casseroles and sauces.

Store frozen stocks, labelled, for up to six months in the freezer.

UTENSILS

The equipment required for soup-making is very basic, and most cooks will already have the required tools in their kitchens. A variety of chopping boards is essential to keep meats and other ingredients separate during food preparation. A variety of sharp vegetable and chopping knives and a vegetable peeler will also be required to make the whole process as easy as possible.

A wire whisk and large sieves are required for blending and straining the soups and large, lidded, heavy-based saucepans in which to make them. The ideal size for most stocks would hold 3 litres/5$^1/_4$ pints/3$^1/_2$ quarts.

Paper towels are used for skimming the scum from the top of the soup, and large spoons for stirring the stocks.

A blender or food processor would be a huge asset for puréed and creamy soups which require the ingredients to be well blended to create a good end result.

The pestle and mortar comes into its own for crushing garlic, peppercorns and other berries and seeds for a really fresh flavour.

ABOUT THE INGREDIENTS

When making your own soup you can be sure that all ingredients are as fresh as possible and in their best condition, that there are no additives and preservatives lurking and no surprise ingredients such as sugars or high salt content. This will add not only an excellent flavour, but will have terrific benefits from a health point of view. Fresh vegetables, meats, fish and fruits are packed with essential vitamins and minerals, protein, carbohydrates and fibre to keep our bodies fighting fit, and a concentrated soup is one of the best ways in which to obtain the recommended daily allowances without feeling you are eating like a rabbit or that eating healthily is a chore.

Generally speaking, soups will make use of a wide range of ingredients, and with yogurt, cream or milk added, recommended calcium allowances will be catered for as well. Throughout the book there is a wide range of soups to cover every occasion, all using fresh ingredients and flavourings such as herbs. Some have creams added to them and, while this gives a good flavour, it may be replaced with natural yogurt for a low-fat alternative.

On a general note, remember to remove excess fat from meats and, when frying is used in the method, be sure to drain the foods well and pat dry with paper towels to reduce the fat content and use olive oil where oil is called for.

When choosing ingredients, look for unblemished fruits and vegetables and where possible use organic produce for a fuller and purer flavour. Store ingredients correctly in the refrigerator if appropriate, and use ingredients as soon after purchase as possible to avoid deterioration.

I hope that you enjoy cooking and eating the soups in the chapters that follow, as much as I have taken pleasure in compiling them. I am sure that from your first tasting you will appreciate the difference in home-made soups as opposed to commercial soups, and will reap the health benefits almost as an aside. Happy soup-making.

There is nothing quite like a bowl of steaming clear soup to start a meal. Light in texture, their most important element is the base. The basic stock recipes given in the introduction are incorporated in this chapter to give a wide range of delicious and stylish recipes using everything from noodles, rice and ravioli to simple fresh vegetables and meats to make up a wide choice of soups. With the easy-to-make recipes, this is one chapter where it would certainly pay to make your stocks in advance and to freeze them in convenient portions. That way you can stir up a soup in minutes by simply adding fresh ingredients.

 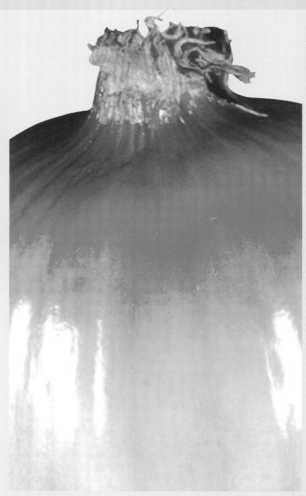

SCOTCH BROTH

Serves 4

675 g/1¹/₂ lb shin of beef
2.5 litres/4¹/₂ pints/2³/₄ quarts basic beef stock (see page 8)
salt and freshly ground black pepper
1 carrot, peeled
1 turnip, peeled
1 leek, sliced
1 red onion, chopped
3 tablespoons pearl barley
1 tablespoon freshly chopped mixed herbs

Remove any fat from the meat and cut the meat into dice. Place in a saucepan and cover with the stock. Season and bring to the boil slowly, cover and simmer for 1¹/₂ hours.

Add the vegetables and barley, cover and simmer for another 1 hour until the vegetables and barley are soft.

Remove any fat from the surface with paper towels. Serve hot, garnished with the mixed herbs.

POTATO AND CARROT SOUP

<u>Serves 4</u>

2 tablespoons sunflower oil
1 small onion, cut into small dice
5 medium-sized carrots, cut into small dice
2 firm or waxy potatoes, cut into small dice
1.5 litres/2¾ pints/7 cups water
salt and freshly ground black pepper
1 teaspoon freshly chopped marjoram
1 teaspoon paprika
⁹/₉ teaspoon brown sugar

Heat the oil in a large saucepan and add the onion. Sauté for 2 minutes, stirring, and add the carrots. Cook for another 3 minutes.

Stir in the potatoes and water and simmer gently for 1 hour or until the vegetables are tender.

Season with salt and pepper and add the remaining ingredients, stirring well, and serve.

VEGETABLE SOUP WITH GINGER

Serves 4

1 litre/1³/₄ pints/4¹/₄ cups basic chicken or vegetable stock
 (see pages 9 and 10)
150 g/5 oz fresh root ginger, peeled
¹/₂ small cauliflower, cut into small florets
2 medium-sized carrots, cut into julienne strips
2 celery sticks, chopped
1 leek, chopped
4 tablespoons single (light) cream (optional)
ground ginger

Place the stock in a large saucepan with the ginger and cook until the ginger is really tender. Remove the ginger from the stock and rub it through a sieve and return to the pan with the remaining vegetables.

Season to taste and simmer until all the vegetables are just tender but not breaking up.

Just before serving, stir in the cream if using. Sprinkle the ground ginger over the top to garnish, then serve.

OLD ENGLISH CABBAGE SOUP

Serves 4

2 leeks, washed
I large brown onion, finely chopped
2 tablespoons butter
400 ml/14 fl oz/1³/4 cups basic chicken stock (see page 9)
I small white cabbage, cored and cut into eight wedges
large pinch of ground cloves
¹/8 teaspoon saffron strands
pinch of mace
¹/2 teaspoon salt
¹/2 teaspoon ground black pepper

Cut the leeks into 5 cm/2 inch pieces. Add to the onion and sauté in the butter in a large saucepan over a low heat until the vegetables have softened.

Add the remaining ingredients and bring to the boil. Reduce the heat and simmer for 30 minutes, or until the cabbage is tender.

Season to taste and serve very hot.

FRESH VEGETABLE SOUP

<u>Serves 4</u>

2 small onions
500 g/18 oz/4 cups mixed vegetables, chopped
2 tablespoons vegetable oil
1 bay leaf
$^1/_2$ teaspoon dried marjoram
$^1/_2$ teaspoon dried thyme
1 litre/1$^3/_4$ pints/4$^1/_4$ cups vegetable stock (see page 10)
salt and freshly ground black pepper

Dice the onions and gently fry in the oil in a large saucepan for 3 minutes, stirring.

Add the mixed vegetables and continue to fry for another 5 minutes. Add the stock and herbs and bring to the boil.

Reduce the heat and simmer for 1 hour, season to taste and serve.

CHICKEN CORN NOODLE SOUP

Serves 4

3 chicken breasts, skinned

400 g/14 oz can creamed sweetcorn

1.25 litres/2¹/₄ pints/5³/₄ cups chicken stock (see page 9)

salt and freshly ground black pepper

2 egg whites

1 tablespoon milk

1 tablespoon cornflour (cornstarch), blended with
  2 tablespoons cold water

6–8 spinach leaves, stalks removed and coarsely shredded

3 spring onions (scallions), finely chopped diagonally

Cut the chicken breasts into long, thin strips. Place the creamed sweetcorn and chicken stock in a large saucepan and bring to the boil.

Add the chicken strips, reduce the heat and simmer gently for 5 minutes. Season with salt and pepper.

Meanwhile whisk the egg whites until they are frothy but not forming peaks and then whisk in the milk.

Stir the cornflour mixture into the soup and bring to the boil, stirring continuously. Add the spinach leaves and spring onions and pour in the egg white mixture.

Stir the soup a few times to allow the egg white to coagulate and to form noodle-like strands on the surface. Serve at once.

RAVIOLI BRODO DI MANZO

Serves 6

2 litres/3¹/₂ pints/2¹/₄ quarts beef stock (see page 8)
125 ml/4 fl oz/¹/₂ cup dry white wine or vermouth
2 tablespoons tomato purée (paste)
1 bay leaf
250 g/9 oz/25–30 small ravioli
freshly ground black pepper
grated Parmesan cheese

Place the stock, wine or vermouth, tomato purée and bay leaf in a large saucepan. Bring to the boil, stirring continuously.

In a separate saucepan, cook the ravioli in plenty of boiling water – a few at a time – until they rise to the surface of the water. Lift the ravioli from the pan with a draining spoon and place in the base of the serving bowls.

Remove the bay leaf from the soup and lightly season the soup to taste. Ladle into the serving bowls and serve with Parmesan cheese.

CONSOMME

Serves 6

1.4 litres/2¹/₂ pints/6¹/₄ cups cold beef stock
 (see page 8)
2 egg whites, lightly beaten
2 egg shells
200 g/7 oz/1³/₄ cups finely minced (ground) beef
2–3 tablespoons sherry or Madeira

Place the stock in a large saucepan with the egg whites, egg shells and beef.

Bring to the boil slowly, whisking occasionally with a wire whisk or fork. Allow the liquid to rise to the top of the pan as it reaches boiling point, then draw the pan aside. Return to the boil, taking care not to break the crust that forms on the top.

Reduce the heat and simmer gently for 30 minutes. Strain the consommé through a sieve (strainer) lined with muslin (cheesecloth), holding the crust back with a slotted draining spoon until all the liquid has been drained from the pan. The consommé should be clear. If not, strain again through the residue remaining in the sieve, into a clean bowl.

Return to the heat, add the sherry or Madeira and serve hot.

Variations

CONSOMME JULIENNE

Cut small pieces of vegetables such as carrot, celery or sweet (bell) peppers and boil separately from the consommé. Drain well and add to the consommé just before serving.

ASPARAGUS CONSOMME

Cook 1 bunch of tender asparagus tips in boiling water for 5 minutes, drain and add to the consommé just before serving.

CONSOMME A LA ROYALE

Make an egg custard by mixing 1 egg yolk, 1 tablespoon stock and seasoning. Strain into a small greased bowl and stand the bowl in a saucepan of hot water. Steam until the custard is firm. Turn it out and cut into strips or shapes, using miniature cutters. Add to the consommé just before serving.

WATERCRESS VEGETABLE SOUP

Serves 6

2 medium-sized carrots
I leek, washed
2 celery sticks
I mignonette lettuce
I tomato
$^1/_2$ cucumber, halved lengthways
60 g/2 oz small mushrooms
36 watercress leaves
2 litres/3$^1/_2$ pints/2$^1/_4$ quarts chicken stock
 (see page 9), simmering
watercress sprigs to garnish

Cut the carrots and leek into fine julienne strips. Cut the celery into thin diagonal slices. Wash the lettuce, choosing six outer dark leaves and six inner lighter leaves. Roll and finely shred the lettuce.

Peel the tomato and remove the seeds. Cut the flesh into small cubes. Scoop the seeds from the cucumber and cut the flesh into tiny cubes. Thinly slice the mushrooms.

Put the carrot, leek and celery into a saucepan of boiling water, cook for 3–4 minutes until tender but still crisp. Drain and refresh in cold water.

Divide the lettuce leaves and watercress leaves between the serving bowls and divide the vegetables between each. Add the tomato, cucumber and mushrooms.

When ready to serve, ladle the chicken stock into the bowls, garnish with watercress sprigs and serve.

CHICKEN AND SWEETCORN

Serves 4

6 spring onions (scallions)
1 red (bell) pepper, seeded and chopped
30 g/1 oz/2 tablespoons butter
400 g/14 oz can sweetcorn
175 g/6 oz cooked lean chicken, shredded
750 ml/1¼ pints/3 cups basic chicken stock (see page 9)
1 egg, beaten

Fry the spring onions and red pepper in the butter in a large saucepan for 30 seconds, stirring. Add the sweetcorn, shredded chicken and stock.

Bring to the boil, reduce the heat and simmer for 10 minutes.

Bring almost to the boil and slowly stir in the beaten egg to form ribbons. Cook until the egg has set, but do not allow the soup to boil.

OXTAIL SOUP

Serves 4

30 g/1 oz butter
2 tablespoons oil
1 oxtail joint
1 onion, chopped
1 carrot, chopped
1 garlic clove, crushed
1.25 litres/2¼ pints/5¾ cups basic beef stock (see page 8)
freshly ground black pepper
1 teaspoon lemon juice
1 tablespoon plain (all-purpose) flour

Melt the butter with the oil and brown the oxtail. Remove the oxtail and place in a large saucepan. Fry the onion, carrot and garlic until browned and add to the oxtail.

Pour the stock into the pan and season well. Bring to the boil, cover and simmer for 5 hours.

Strain the soup and skim off the excess fat. Return the strained soup to the pan, add the lemon juice and reheat.

Mix the flour to a paste with a little cold water and stir into the soup. Cook gently for 2–3 minutes until the soup thickens. Serve.

VEGETABLE POTTAGE

Serves 4

60 g/2 oz/¹/₂ cup butter
1 red onion, sliced
4 carrots, chopped
125 g/4 oz/1¹/₂ cup swede (rutabaga), chopped
2 celery sticks, sliced
1.25 litres/2¹/₄ pints/5³/₄ cups basic vegetable stock
(see page 10)
salt and freshly ground black pepper
freshly chopped thyme to garnish

Melt the butter in a large saucepan and cook the onion until softened but not brown. Add the carrots, swede and celery and sauté for 4 minutes more.

Stir in the stock and season to taste. Bring to the boil, reduce the heat, cover and simmer for 1¹/₂ hours, or until the vegetables are tender.

Adjust the seasoning, garnish and serve.

MUSSEL SOUP

Serves 4

1 kg/2¼ lb mussels
250 ml/8 fl oz/1 cup dry white wine
2 leeks, sliced
2 carrots, diced
½ small fennel bulb, chopped
60 g/2 oz/¼ cup butter
1 litre/1¾ pints/4¼ cups basic fish stock (see page 9)
salt and freshly ground black pepper
celery leaves to garnish

Clean the mussels well and discard any that are open. Place the closed mussels in a large saucepan with the wine, cover and simmer for several minutes until the mussels open.

Remove the mussels from the pan and remove from their shells. Discard any unopened mussels. Strain the wine through muslin (cheesecloth) and reserve.

Melt the butter in a large saucepan and cook the leeks, carrot and fennel for 15 minutes until softened. Add the stock and mussel cooking liquid, season and simmer for 20 minutes.

Add the mussels to the pan and stir until thoroughly heated through. Serve immediately, garnished with celery leaves.

MOCK TURTLE SOUP

Serves 4

1 litre/1³/₄ pints/4¹/₄ cups basic beef stock (see page 8)
2 egg whites
juice and rind of 1 small lemon
15 g/¹/₂ oz/¹/₄ cup mixed herbs, tied in a muslin bag
3 peppercorns
60 g/2 oz/¹/₂ cup carrots, chopped
60 g/2 oz/¹/₂ cup celery, chopped
2 tablespoons cornflour (cornstarch)
salt
3–4 tablespoons Madeira or sherry

Place all the ingredients except the salt and Madeira in a large saucepan and bring to the boil two or three times. Remove from the heat and leave to infuse for 30 minutes.

Strain twice through a double thickness of muslin (cheesecloth) to give a clear liquid.

Reheat the soup without allowing it to boil and season to taste. Stir in the Madeira and serve immediately.

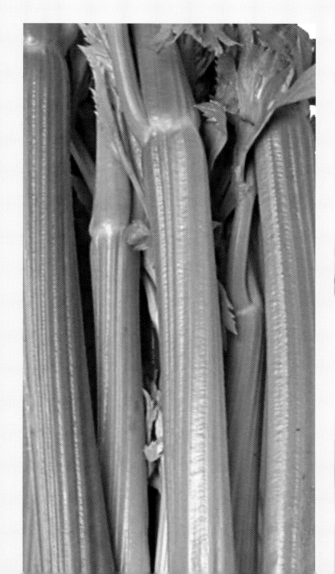

CHINESE RICE SOUP

Serves 4

60 g/2 oz/³/₄ cup dried Chinese mushrooms
1 litre/1³/₄ pints/4¹/₄ cups basic chicken stock (see page 9)
450 g/1 lb beancurd, cut into cubes
6 spring onions (scallions), finely chopped
2 tablespoons dry sherry
1 tablespoon light soy sauce
few drops of chilli oil
2 rice cakes
oil for frying

Soak the dried mushrooms in warm water for 20 minutes. Drain and squeeze out any excess liquid. Shred the mushrooms into thin strips and reserve.

Place the stock in a large saucepan and bring to simmering point. Add the remaining soup ingredients, apart from the rice cake and oil, simmer for 20 minutes.

Meanwhile, break the rice cakes into eight and heat the oil for frying in a wok. Fry the cakes for 1 minute until lightly browned. Remove from the oil with a draining spoon and pat dry on paper towels.

Place two pieces of rice cake in the base of each serving dish and spoon the soup over the top. Serve immediately.

FRENCH ONION SOUP

Serves 6

60 g/2 oz/¼ cup butter
1 tablespoon oil
675 g/1½ lb onions, thinly sliced
1 tablespoon salt
15 g/1½ oz/2 tablespoons plain (all-purpose) flour
2 litres/3½ pints/2¼ quarts basic beef stock
 (see page 8), boiling
125 ml/4 fl oz/½ cup dry white wine or vermouth
freshly ground black pepper
12 thick French bread slices
125 g/4 oz/½ cup butter, melted
2–3 tablespoons brandy
200 g/7 oz/1¾ cups Gruyère or mature (sharp)
 Cheddar cheese, coarsely grated

Melt the butter in a large saucepan. Add the
oil and onions and cook, uncovered, over a
low heat for 20 minutes, stirring occasionally,
until a rich golden colour.

Be careful not to burn the onions. Sprinkle
with salt and flour and stir over a moderate
heat for 3 minutes. Remove from the heat and
stir in the boiling stock, gradually. Add the
wine or vermouth and season with pepper.
Return to the heat, cover and simmer for
30–40 minutes.

Brush the bread with melted butter on both
sides. Place in a single layer in a shallow
ovenproof dish and bake in a preheated oven
at 160°C/325°F/Gas 3 for 20 minutes, or
until lightly brown and dried out.

Just before serving, season and stir in the
brandy. Ladle into serving bowls and top each
with 2 bread slices. Sprinkle with the cheese.

NOODLE SOUP

Serves 4

225 g/8 oz dried Chinese egg noodles
1 litre/1³/₄ pints/4¹/₄ cups basic vegetable stock
 (see page 10)
2 spring onions (scallions), finely chopped
1 stalk lemon grass, finely chopped
2 tablespoons freshly chopped parsley
2 celery sticks, finely chopped
1 teaspoon sesame oil
2 teaspoons chilli oil
1 tablespoon lemon juice
1 tablespoon light soy sauce
2 teaspoons brown sugar

Cook the noodles in boiling water for 4–5 minutes until cooked. Drain and reserve.

Pour the stock into a large saucepan and bring to simmering point. Add the remaining ingredients and simmer for 5 minutes.

Stir the noodles into the soup and return to simmering point. Serve immediately.

PASTA IN BROTH

Serves 6

1.25 litres/2^1/$_4$ pints/5^3/$_4$ cups basic chicken stock
(see page 9)
400 g/14 oz/3^1/$_2$ dried pasta shapes
1 red (red) pepper, seeded and chopped
freshly grated Parmesan cheese to garnish

Bring the stock to the boil in a large saucepan and add the pasta shapes and pepper. Cook for 8–10 minutes until the pasta is cooked.

Ladle the soup into serving bowls and garnish with grated Parmesan cheese.

By adding single (light), double (heavy) or soured creams, natural yogurt or crème fraîche to soups as a final step before serving, the flavours are transformed and a richness and smoothness given to them, which differentiates them from other recipes in this book. Most creamy soups are blended for smoothness and contain an ingredient such as potato or other starches to achieve the required texture. To reduce the fat content of these recipes, use yogurt in place of the creams, but do not boil the soups once this has been added, as it will curdle.

CELERIAC SOUP

Serves 4

2 tablespoons butter
30 g/1 oz/2 medium-sized onions, sliced
2 large celeriac roots about 1 kg (2¼ lb) trimmed weight
450 g/1 lb potatoes
1 teaspoon salt
½ teaspoon celery seed
750 ml/1¼ pints/3 cups water
475 ml/16 fl oz/2 cups milk
white pepper to taste

Melt the butter in a large casserole over a low heat. Add the onions, cover and cook until golden brown, about 10 minutes. Stir occasionally.

Wash and peel the celeriac and cut into thick slices. Add to the onions with the potatoes, salt and celery seed, stirring well to coat with the butter. Add the water and milk, cover the casserole and simmer until the vegetables are tender, about 30 minutes.

Transfer the mixture to a food processor in batches and purée for a few seconds, retaining some of the chunky texture. Return the soup to the casserole, season with white pepper and reheat gently. Add a little more milk if the soup is too thick.

OLD-FASHIONED CREAM OF TOMATO SOUP

<u>Serves 4-6</u>

1 small brown onion, finely chopped
30 g/1 oz/2 tablespoons butter
30 g/1 oz/¼ cup (all-purpose) flour
250 ml/8 fl oz/1 cup milk
675 g/1½ lb/5 cups fresh tomatoes, peeled and chopped
1 teaspoon fresh thyme
5 basil leaves, chopped
475 ml/16 fl oz/2 cups single (light) cream

In a large saucepan, sauté the onion in the butter for 2 minutes, then add the flour. Stir and cook for 2 minutes more.

Whisk the milk into the pan, whisking constantly until the mixture thickens. Add the tomatoes and their juices and simmer for 10 minutes, or until pulpy.

Transfer the mixture to a food processor and blend until really smooth. Return the soup to the pan, add the herbs and seasoning and stir in the cream. Heat through thoroughly, but do not allow the soup to boil.

PEA AND CUCUMBER

Serves 4-6

225 g/8 oz/1¹/₂ cups pre-cooked or frozen peas
1 large potato, sliced
¹/₂ Spanish red onion, sliced
1 litre/1³/₄ pints/4¹/₄ cups basic chicken stock (see page 9)
30 g/1 oz/2 tablespoons butter
125 ml/4 fl oz/¹/₂ cup water
1 cucumber, peeled and seeded
150 ml/¹/₄ pint/²/₃ cup single (light) cream
2 egg yolks, lightly beaten
salt and freshly ground black pepper
sprigs of mint

Combine the peas, potato and onion in a saucepan. Add 350 ml/12 fl oz/1¹/₂ cups of the chicken stock and half of the butter. Simmer for 20 minutes until the vegetables are tender. Allow to cool and transfer to a food processor. Add the water and blend until smooth.

Cut the cucumber into matchsticks and cook in the remaining butter until tender. Add the cream and beaten egg yolks to the vegetable purée and mix well.

Heat the remaining chicken stock in a large saucepan and add the vegetable purée, cooking over a low heat until the soup is smooth and thick. Do not boil, otherwise the egg yolks will curdle.

Season to taste and add the cucumber matchsticks. Garnish with mint sprigs and serve immediately.

COUNTRY PUMPKIN SOUP

Serves 4

450 g/1 lb pumpkin, peeled and cut into chunks
1 brown onion, sliced
1.25 litres/2^1/$_4$ pints/5^3/$_4$ cups water
^{1}/$_2$ teaspoon salt
150 ml/^{1}/$_4$ pint/^{2}/$_3$ cup orange juice
150 ml/^{1}/$_4$ pint/^{2}/$_3$ cup single (light) cream
2 teaspoons curry powder

Put the pumpkin, onion and salt into a large saucepan with the water. Cover and bring to the boil. Boil for 15 minutes, or until the pumpkin is soft. Drain, reserving the liquid, and transfer the pumpkin flesh and onion to a food processor. Blend until smooth.

Add 150 ml/^{1}/$_4$ pint/^{2}/$_3$ cup of the cooking liquid together with the orange juice, cream and curry powder to the purée and blend again until really smooth.

Either reheat the soup gently in a clean pan, but do not allow it to boil, or chill in the refrigerator and serve cold.

CREAM OF PARSLEY SOUP

Serves 8

75 g/2¹/₂ oz/2 cups parsley
I large brown onion, sliced
4 celery sticks, washed and sliced thinly
30 g/I oz/2 tablespoons butter or margarine
3 tablespoons plain (all-purpose) flour
1.8 litres/3 pints/2 quarts basic chicken stock (see page 9)
salt and freshly ground black pepper
125 ml/4 fl oz/¹/₂ cup single (light) cream
sprigs of parsley to garnish

Wash the parsley and drain off any excess water, roughly chop and mix with the onion and celery.

Melt the butter or margarine in a large saucepan and add the vegetables. Cover and cook the vegetables over a medium heat until quite soft, about 10 minutes.

Stir in the flour to make a smooth paste, then stir in the stock and season to taste.

Bring the mixture to the boil, cover and reduce the heat to a simmer. Cook for 25–30 minutes, then allow to cool.

Transfer the mixture to a food processor and blend until smooth.

Return the soup to a clean saucepan and heat through thoroughly. Swirl in the cream and serve garnished with parsley.

CURRIED PARSNIP AND ORANGE SOUP

Serves 4

2 tablespoons butter or margarine
2 medium-sized parsnips, thinly sliced
1 medium-sized brown onion, chopped
1 garlic clove, crushed
1 teaspoon curry powder
1 teaspoon ground cumin
1 tablespoon plain (all-purpose) flour
1.25 litres/2¼ pints/5¾ cups basic chicken stock
(see page 9)
finely grated rind and the juice of 2 oranges
salt and freshly ground black pepper to taste
125 ml/4 fl oz/½ cup single (light) cream

Melt the butter or margarine in a large saucepan and fry the parsnips and onion until soft, about 10 minutes. Keep the lid on and shake the saucepan throughout cooking.

Add the garlic and spices and cook, uncovered, for 2 minutes more.

While stirring, add the flour and cook for another 2 minutes, then pour in the stock and orange juice. Bring to the boil and season to taste.

Lower the heat, cover the saucepan and simmer for about 20 minutes until all the vegetables are tender. Allow to cool.

Transfer the soup to a food processor and blend until smooth. Refrigerate the soup, covered, for 12 hours.

To reheat the soup, stir in half of the cream and heat through without boiling. Ladle into soup bowls and swirl in the remaining cream. Sprinkle with grated orange rind and serve.

SMOKED FISH SOUP

Serves 4

750 g/1³/₄ lb smoked fish fillets
1 brown onion, thinly sliced and separated into rings
750 ml/1¹/₄ pints/3 cups milk
2 medium-sized potatoes, cooked and mashed
2 bay leaves
pinch of ground nutmeg
white pepper
150 ml/¹/₄ pint/²/₃ cup single (light) cream
1 tablespoon freshly chopped parsley

Place the smoked fish fillets in a greased baking dish and top with the onion rings. Pour just enough water into the dish to cover the fish and onions. Cover the dish with baking foil and cook in a preheated oven at 180°C/350°F/Gas 4 for 20 minutes, or until the fish is tender. Drain and reserve the liquid and fish, discarding the onion.

Remove any skin and bones from the fish and flake the flesh.

In a separate saucepan, combine the milk and mashed potatoes, stirring over a low heat until the mixture comes to the boil and has a creamy smooth texture. Add the reserved fish cooking liquid and bay leaves and simmer for 5 minutes.

Remove the bay leaves from the pan and discard. Add the fish to the pan, season with nutmeg and pepper and stir in the cream. Heat through, but do not allow the soup to boil, otherwise the cream will curdle.

Ladle into warmed soup bowls and sprinkle with the chopped parsley.

SPICY COCONUT PEANUT SOUP

Serves 4-6

1 tablespoon peanut oil
1 onion, finely chopped
4 garlic cloves, crushed
1¹/₂ tablespoon grated fresh root ginger
1 teaspoon ground turmeric
1 teaspoon ground coriander
1 teaspoon curry paste
250 g/9 oz/1¹/₄ cups potatoes, peeled and chopped
750 ml/1¹/₄ pints/3 cups basic chicken stock (see page 9)
250 ml/8 fl oz/1 cup coconut milk
¹/₂ Chinese cabbage, finely shredded
3 tablespoons crunchy peanut butter
2 tablespoons soy sauce
juice of 1 lime
1 teaspoon brown sugar
spring onions (scallions), finely chopped

Heat the oil in a large saucepan. Add the onion, garlic and ginger and sauté for 1 minute. Add the turmeric, coriander, curry paste and potato. Cook for 1–2 minutes, stirring continuously.

Add the stock and coconut milk and simmer for 10–12 minutes, until the potato is tender. Add the cabbage and return the mixture to the boil.

Reduce the heat to a simmer and cook for 2 minutes only. Remove from the heat. Stir a little of the soup into the peanut butter with the soy sauce, lime juice and sugar. Add this mixture to the soup, and adjust the seasonings to taste. Garnish with spring onions and serve immediately.

CREAM OF PEA AND LETTUCE

Serves 6-8

30 g/1 oz/2 tablespoons butter
1 large onion
500 g/18 oz/3 cups shelled or frozen peas
1 red eating apple, peeled and cut into cubes
$^1/_2$ large iceberg lettuce or 1 butter lettuce, finely sliced
1.5 litres/2$^3/_4$ pints/7 cups basic chicken stock (see page 9)
salt and freshly ground black pepper
a pinch of ground nutmeg
2 egg yolks
125 ml/4 fl oz/$^1/_2$ cup single (light) cream
fried croûtons (see page 147)
mustard and cress or chopped mint to garnish

Melt the butter in a large saucepan, add the onion and sauté for 3 minutes until softened. Add the peas and stir continuously until they are shiny and green.

Stir in the apple, lettuce and stock and bring the mixture to the boil. Reduce the heat to a simmer and cook for 15–20 minutes until the peas are tender, if fresh, or 10–12 minutes if peas are frozen.

Transfer the soup to a food processor and blend until smooth. Season with salt and pepper and add the ground nutmeg.

Mix the egg yolks with the cream in a mixing bowl. Quickly stir in about 250 ml/8 fl oz/ 1 cup of the soup, then return to the saucepan. Stir over a low heat, but do not boil. Adjust the seasonings to taste and serve immediately, scattered with croûtons, mustard and cress or mint.

SUNSET CREAM

Serves 6

30 g/1 oz/2 tablespoons butter
2 onions, finely chopped
2 tablespoons plain (all-purpose) flour, sifted
1 kg/2¹/₄ lb ripe tomatoes, peeled and finely chopped
1 teaspoon salt
2 teaspoons caster (superfine) sugar
¹/₄–¹/₂ teaspoon cracked peppercorns
¹/₂ teaspoon dried sage, basil or oregano
1 bay leaf
1.15 litres/2 pints/5 cups water
1–2 tablespoons tomato purée (paste), optional
single (light) cream to garnish
freshly chopped parsley to garnish

Melt the butter in a large saucepan and cook the onions for 5 minutes, stirring regularly until softened. Stir in the flour and cook for about 3 minutes.

Add the tomatoes, salt, sugar, dried herbs and bay leaf. Bring to the boil, then reduce the heat and simmer for 15 minutes.

Add the water and simmer for another 15 minutes. Remove the bay leaf and discard. Transfer the soup to a food processor and blend until smooth.

Return to a clean saucepan and bring back to the boil. Adjust the seasoning, adding the tomato purée if using. Ladle into soup bowls and serve with a swirl of cream and chopped parsley to garnish.

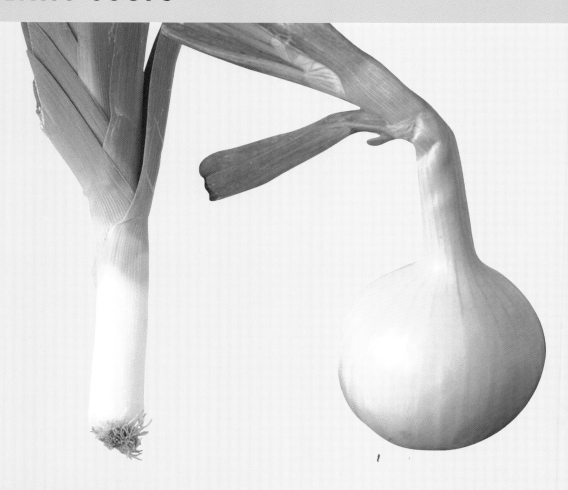

CREAMY SORREL SOUP

Serves 4

30 g/1 oz/2 tablespoons butter
1 onion, thinly sliced
2 leeks, thinly sliced
500 g/18 oz/6 cups shredded sorrel leaves
pinch of freshly grated nutmeg
salt and freshly ground black pepper
2 potatoes, sliced
1.15 litres/2 pints/5 cups basic vegetable stock (see page 10)
5 tablespoons single (light) cream
1 tablespoon freshly chopped chervil

Melt the butter in a large saucepan and fry the onion for 2–3 minutes until softened. Add the leeks and sorrel and stir well. Season with salt, pepper and nutmeg. Cover and simmer gently for 5 minutes.

Add the potatoes and simmer for another 5 minutes, stirring occasionally.

Add the stock, cover and simmer for 30 minutes, or until the vegetables are tender.

Transfer the soup to a food processor and blend until smooth. Return the soup to the cleaned pan and heat through thoroughly.

Ladle the soup into serving bowls and swirl the cream on to the top. Sprinkle with the chopped chervil and serve.

CHICKEN SOUP

Serves 4

15 g/¹/₂ oz/1 tablespoon butter
1 chicken quarter
1 garlic clove, crushed
1 bay leaf
1 thyme sprig
2 parsley sprigs
1 onion, chopped
1 celery stick, diced
pared rind and juice of 1 lemon
1.15 litres/2 pints/5 cups basic chicken stock (see page 9)
salt and freshly ground black pepper
200 ml/7 fl oz/³/₄ cup single (light) cream
croûtons (see page 147)
2 tablespoons freshly chopped parsley
6 black olives, stoned (pitted) and chopped

Melt the butter in a large saucepan. Add the chicken quarter and brown it all over. Add the garlic, bay leaf, thyme and parsley, vegetables and lemon rind. Cover and cook for 15 minutes.

Pour in the stock and bring to the boil. Reduce the heat, cover and simmer for 45 minutes. Lift the chicken from the pan and remove the skin. Dice the chicken meat. Remove the herbs from the soup and discard. Transfer the soup to a food processor and blend to a purée or rub through a sieve (strainer) into a bowl.

To reheat the soup, return to a clean saucepan, add the chicken, lemon juice and seasoning. Reduce the heat to a minimum and stir in the cream. Heat for a moment and remove from the heat.

Ladle the soup into serving bowls. Mix the croûtons, chopped parsley and chopped olives together and sprinkle a little onto each serving. Serve the remaining croûton mixture separately.

CORIANDER SOUP

Serves 6

1 tablespoon butter
1 tablespoon olive oil
2 celery sticks, chopped
1 onion, chopped
2 teaspoons grated root ginger
1 garlic clove, crushed
1 tablespoon plain (all-purpose) flour
900 ml/1½ pints/3¾ quarts basic chicken stock
 (see page 9), heated
30 g/1 oz/½ cup fresh coriander (cilantro) leaves
salt and freshly ground black pepper
250 ml/8 fl oz/1 cup soured cream
lemon juice
a few coriander leaves to garnish

Heat the butter and oil in a large saucepan and sauté the celery, onion, ginger and garlic for 3–4 minutes until softened. Sprinkle the flour over the top and slowly stir in the heated stock.

Bring to the boil, stirring, then reduce the heat and simmer for 10 minutes.

Remove from the heat and stir in the coriander leaves and seasoning. Leave the soup to stand for 10 minutes.

If serving hot, reheat gently and then stir in the soured cream just before serving, garnished with coriander leaves. To serve cold, cover and chill in the refrigerator overnight and stir in the cream before serving.

CREAMY MUSHROOM SOUP

Serves 4

225 g/8 oz/3 cups open cap mushrooms, chopped
2 celery sticks, chopped
1 garlic clove, crushed
1.25 litres/2^1/$_4$ pints/5^3/$_4$ cups basic vegetable stock
 (see page 10)
600 ml/1 pint/2^1/$_2$ cups milk
salt and freshly ground black pepper
1 tablespoon plain (all-purpose) flour
freshly chopped parsley to garnish

Place the mushrooms, celery and garlic in a large saucepan with the stock and bring to the boil. Reduce the heat and simmer for 15 minutes until the vegetables are tender.

Reserving 1 tablespoon of the milk, add the rest to the stock and season to taste. Return the soup to the boil.

Blend the flour with the reserved milk and stir into the soup. Simmer for 3–4 minutes until the soup thickens, sprinkle with parsley and serve.

CREAM OF LOBSTER SOUP

Serves 4

450 g/1 lb lobster shells
60 g/2 oz/¹/₄ cup butter
1 onion, chopped
1 carrot, chopped
1 garlic clove, crushed
1 celery stick, chopped
1 tablespoon brandy
1 tablespoon tomato purée (paste)
150 ml/¹/₄ pint/²/₃ cup vermouth
1 litre/1³/₄ pints/4¹/₄ cups basic fish stock (see page 9)
1 bouquet garni
60 g/2 oz/¹/₂ cup rice flour
salt and freshly ground black pepper
150 g/5 oz/1 cup lobster meat
150 ml/¹/₄ pint/²/₃ cup single (light) cream

Break the shells into pieces. Melt the butter in a large saucepan and add the shells, onion, carrot, garlic and celery. Cook gently until softened.

In a separate saucepan, warm the brandy and ignite. Allow the flames to extinguish before pouring the brandy over the vegetables. Add the tomato purée, vermouth, stock and bouquet garni, and bring to the boil.

Reduce the heat to a simmer and cook for 15–20 minutes. Mix the rice flour with a little cold water and add to the soup. Return the soup to the boil until it thickens.

Remove the shells from the soup and discard. Cook for another 20 minutes.

Strain the soup and return to the pan. Bring to the boil and add the seasoning and lobster meat and stir in the cream. Heat through, but do not allow the soup to boil. Serve immediately.

CREAM OF CELERY SOUP

Serves 4

1 head celery, sliced
1 leek, sliced
30 g/1 oz/2 tablespoons butter
500 ml/17 fl oz/2¹/₄ cups basic vegetable stock (see page 10)
salt and freshly ground black pepper
250 ml/ 8 fl oz/1 cup milk
2 tablespoons double (heavy) cream or natural yogurt
freshly chopped parsley to garnish

Fry the vegetables in the butter in a saucepan for about 10 minutes or until softened but not browned.

Add the stock and season to taste. Bring to the boil, cover and simmer for 25 minutes until the vegetables are tender.

Press the soup through a sieve and return the liquid to a clean pan. Stir in the milk, bring to the boil and then simmer for 5 minutes. Stir the cream or yogurt into the soup and serve immediately, garnished with parsley.

JULIENNE OF VEGETABLES

<u>Serves 4</u>

30 g/1 oz/2 tablespoons butter
1 leek, shredded
2 carrots, cut into julienne strips
3 celery sticks, sliced
125 g/4 oz swede (rutabaga), cut into julienne strips
1.8 litres/3 pints/2 quarts basic vegetable stock (see page 10)
salt and freshly ground black pepper
1 tablespoon freshly chopped parsley
2 tablespoons single (light) cream

Melt the butter in a large saucepan and fry the vegetables until golden brown. Add the stock and bring to the boil. Cover and simmer for 1 hour.

Transfer the soup to a food processor and blend until smooth. Return the soup to a clean saucepan and season to taste.

Stir in the parsley and the cream. Heat through thoroughly, but do not allow to boil. Ladle into serving bowls and serve immediately.

CREAM OF CARROT SOUP

Serves 4

30 g/1 oz/2 tablespoons butter
225 g/8 oz/1½ cups carrots, grated
1 large potato, grated
600 ml/1 pint/2½ cups basic vegetable stock (see page 10)
600 ml/1 pint/2½ cups milk
2 tablespoons long-grain rice
pinch of ground ginger
salt and freshly ground black pepper
2 teaspoons orange juice
3 tablespoons single (light) cream
freshly chopped coriander (cilantro) to garnish

Melt the butter in a large saucepan and sauté the carrots and potato for 5 minutes, stirring.

Add the stock, milk, rice and ground ginger, and season to taste. Bring to the boil, reduce the heat, cover and simmer for 30 minutes or until the rice is cooked.

Stir in the orange juice and cream – do not allow the soup to boil. Sprinkle the chopped coriander over the top and serve.

CREAMY BLUE CHEESE SOUP

Serves 4

30 g/1 oz/2 tablespoons butter
1 red onion, chopped
4 leeks, sliced
30 g/1 oz/¼ cup plain (all-purpose) flour
475 ml/16 fl oz/2 cups basic chicken stock (see page 9)
2 tablespoons freshly chopped mixed herbs
475 ml/16 fl oz/2 cups milk
120 g/4 oz/1 cup blue cheese, crumbled
freshly ground black pepper
3–4 tablespoons yogurt

Melt the butter in a large saucepan, add the onion and leeks and sauté for 5 minutes, stirring constantly.

Stir in the flour and cook for 1 minute. Gradually stir in the stock and bring to the boil, stirring until the soup thickens.

Add the herbs and simmer for 20 minutes.

Allow the soup to cool slightly and transfer to a food processor. Blend until smooth and return to a clean saucepan. Add the milk and heat until almost boiling.

Remove from the heat and stir in the cheese and yogurt, stirring until the cheese has melted. Serve immediately.

OYSTER AND BEER SOUP

Serves 4

For the velouté
45 g/1¹/₂ oz/3 tablespoons butter
45 g/1¹/₂ oz/¹/₃ cup plain (all-purpose) flour
600 ml/1 pint/2¹/₂ cups milk
600 ml/1 pint/2¹/₂ cups basic fish stock (see page 9)
For the soup
30 g/1 oz/2 tablespoons butter
1 small onion, chopped
150 ml/¹/₄ pint/²/₃ cup vermouth
12 oysters
300 ml/¹/₂ pint/1¹/₄ cups stout
150 ml/¹/₄ pint/²/₃ cup double (heavy) cream
freshly chopped parsley to garnish

Melt the butter for the velouté in a saucepan and add the flour. Cook for 1 minute. Gradually whisk in the milk and stock and bring to the boil until it begins to thicken.

Melt the butter for the soup in a large saucepan and cook the onion for 5 minutes, or until softened. Add the vermouth and bring to the boil.

Gradually stir in the prepared velouté and bring to the boil. Simmer for 15 minutes.

Open the oysters and add their juices to the soup. Stir in the stout, bring back to the boil, then reduce the heat and pour in the cream. Sieve the soup and return to the pan.

Gently heat the soup without boiling and add the oysters. Cook for 2–3 minutes and serve immediately, garnished with parsley.

CAULIFLOWER SOUP GRATIN

Serves 4

1 cauliflower
1 litre/1³/₄ pints/4¹/₄ cups basic chicken stock (see page 9)
150 ml/¹/₄ pint/²/₃ cup milk or single (light) cream
30 g/1 oz/2 tablespoons butter
salt and freshly ground black pepper
¹/₂ teaspoon ground nutmeg
1–2 egg yolks
125 g/4 oz/1 cup Gruyère or Cheddar cheese, grated
60 g/2 oz/¹/₂ cup plain dried bread crumbs
freshly chopped parsley to garnish

Remove the outer leaves from the cauliflower and the thick central stalk. Cut off the florets and the smallest leaves. Cook them in boiling water until tender, drain thoroughly and purée in a food processor.

Return the purée to the clean saucepan, add the stock and bring to the boil slowly. Stir in the milk or cream, butter and seasonings.

Beat the egg yolks with a little extra cold milk or water in a bowl. Quickly stir in about 250 ml/8 fl oz/1 cup of hot soup, then return the egg mixture to the saucepan. Stir over a low heat but do not boil, otherwise the egg yolks will curdle.

Mix the cheese and bread crumbs in a bowl. Ladle the soup into four ovenproof 250 ml/ 8 fl oz/1 cup soup bowls and stand them on a baking sheet. Sprinkle the cheese mixture over the top and cook under a medium grill (broiler) until the cheese melts. Garnish with parsley and serve immediately.

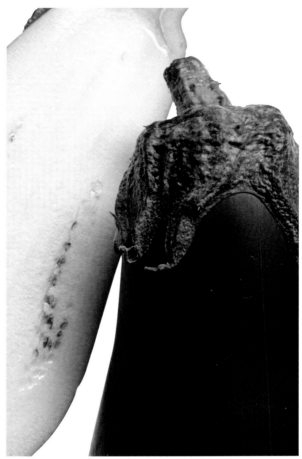

CREAMY AUBERGINE SOUP

Serves 4

350 g/12 oz aubergine (eggplant)
225 g/8 oz canned tomatoes
1 large onion
1 green chilli, seeded
900 ml/1½ pints/3¾ cups basic chicken stock (see page 9)
400 ml/14 fl oz/1¾ cups coconut milk
2 tablespoons olive oil
2 garlic cloves, crushed
2 teaspoons sugar
freshly ground black pepper

Peel and cut the aubergine into cubes. Cut the tomatoes into small chunks. Finely chop the onion and chilli.

Place the stock and coconut milk in a large saucepan and bring to the boil, then reduce the heat and simmer. Heat the oil in a large frying pan (skillet) and sauté the onion, garlic, chilli and aubergine for 4 minutes, stirring. Drain on paper towels and add to the stock mixture.

Add the remaining ingredients and cook for 5–10 minutes. Serve immediately.

Puréed soups are generally
wholesome, thicker soups and are
prepared from any root or green
vegetable, or pulses and lentils are added. The
vegetables are sautéed first in oil, cooked in
stock and then puréed to the required
texture. If you prefer, reserve a few vegetable
pieces before blending and return them to the
soup to serve. This gives the soup some
interest visually and gives it texture.

GREEN BEAN SOUP

Serves 4

30 g/1 oz/2 tablespoons butter
450 g/1 lb runner beans
2 onions, chopped
1 garlic clove, crushed
1 carrot, chopped
1 celery stick, chopped
900 ml/1½ pints/3¾ cups basic vegetable stock
 (see page 10)
salt and cayenne pepper

Melt the butter in a large saucepan and sauté the vegetables for 10 minutes, until softened but not browned.

Add the stock and bring to the boil. Reduce the heat, cover and simmer for 30 minutes until the vegetables are tender.

Transfer the mixture to a food processor and blend until smooth. Return the soup to a clean saucepan and season to taste. Heat through thoroughly and serve.

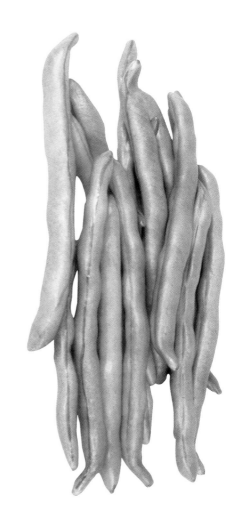

CHERVIL SOUP

Serves 4-6

15 g/¹/₂ oz/1 tablespoon butter
125 g/4 oz/²/₃ cup potato, peeled and diced
1 leek, sliced
1 small onion, sliced
1.25 litres/2¹/₄ pints/ 5³/₄ cups basic chicken stock
(see page 9)
1 tablespoon cornflour (cornstarch)
2 tablespoons milk
salt and freshly ground black pepper
1¹/₂ tablespoon finely chopped chervil

Melt the butter in a large saucepan and add the potato, leek and onion. Cook, stirring gently until the onion is softened, about 3 minutes.

Add the stock and simmer for 30 minutes. Transfer the mixture to a food processor and blend until smooth. Return the soup to a clean saucepan.

Cook over a low heat. Mix the cornflour with the milk and add to the soup. Bring to the boil until the soup thickens. Season to taste.

Just before serving, add the chopped chervil to the soup, stirring well. Ladle into soup bowls and serve.

POTATO AND ONION SOUP

Serves 4

450 g/1 lb potatoes
4 small onions, finely sliced
125 g/4 oz/¹/₂ cup butter
60 g/2 oz/¹/₂ cup plain (all-purpose) flour
750 ml/1¹/₄ pints/3 cups basic vegetable stock (see page 10)
150 ml/¹/₄ pint/²/₃ cup milk
salt and freshly ground black pepper
1 tablespoon chopped parsley to garnish

Boil the potatoes in salted water for 20 minutes. Drain thoroughly then peel and mash until smooth.

In a heavy-based large saucepan, sauté the onions in the butter over a low heat for 5 minutes or until softened.

Add the flour and stir to make a thick paste, then gradually stir in the hot stock. Bring to the boil and allow to simmer for 5 minutes.

Add the potato to the pan and simmer for another 5 minutes before adding the milk. Season with salt and pepper and blend in a food processor to liquidize all the ingredients. Ladle into soup bowls, garnish with parsley and serve.

MASHED POTATO AND THYME SOUP

Serves 4

15 g/¹/₂ oz/1 tablespoon butter
1 onion, finely chopped
2 spring onions (scallions), white part only, thinly sliced
3 shallots, very finely chopped
900 ml/1¹/₂ pints/3³/₄ cups basic vegetable stock
 (see page 10)
2 teaspoons dried thyme
450 g/1 lb potatoes, cooked and mashed
4 tablespoons dry white wine
salt and freshly ground black pepper
3 tablespoons snipped chives to garnish

Melt the butter in a large saucepan and add the onion, spring onions and shallots. Cook for 3–4 minutes until softened but not browned.

Stir in the stock and thyme and bring to the boil. Gradually add the mashed potato and return the soup to the boil.

Reduce the heat to low, stir in the wine and simmer for 5 minutes. Season generously and ladle into soup bowls. Serve garnished with the chives.

BEETROOT SOUP

Serves 4-6

2 leeks, washed

450 g/1 lb potatoes, quartered

1.15 litres/2 pints/5 cups basic chicken stock (see page 9)

1 large beetroot, peeled and cut into chunks

4 tablespoons butter

3–4 tablespoons single (light) cream

Slice the white part of the leeks, discarding the rest, and cook gently in a large saucepan, in 1 tablespoon of the butter until softened but not browned. Add the potatoes and stock and simmer for 15–20 minutes until the potatoes are tender. Transfer the mixture to a food processor and blend until smooth. Return to the cleaned saucepan.

Cook the beetroot in a preheated oven at 180°C/350°F/Gas mark 4 with 1 tablespoon of the butter until tender. Remove from the oven and blend until smooth in a food processor. Stir the beetroot into the potato in the pan, mixing well.

Cook over a low heat and dilute with a little stock if the soup is too thick.

Stir in the remaining butter and the cream just before serving.

CAULIFLOWER AND GINGER SOUP

Serves 8

1 large cauliflower
1 large onion, finely chopped
1 tablespoon butter or margarine
1 tablespoon vegetable oil
1 tablespoon freshly chopped root ginger
1 litre/1³/₄ pints/4¹/₄ cups basic vegetable stock
 (see page 10)
salt and freshly ground black pepper

Remove the base of the cauliflower and discard with the outer leaves. Thinly slice the remaining leaves and break the cauliflower into florets. Wash and drain.

Heat the butter or margarine and the oil in a large saucepan and add the vegetables. Cover and cook for 10 minutes, stirring the vegetables occasionally to prevent browning.

Add the ginger and stock and season to taste. Cover and simmer for another 30 minutes until the vegetables are tender.

Allow the soup to cool before transferring to a food processor. Blend until smooth and return the soup to the cleaned saucepan. Reheat gently and ladle into warmed soup bowls to serve.

CELERY AND APRICOT SOUP

Serves 6

1 head of celery, tops removed
1 teaspoon margarine
1 tablespoon oil
1 large onion, chopped
90 g/3 oz/$^1/_2$ cup no-need-to-soak dried apricots, chopped
1 litre/1$^3/_4$ pints/4$^1/_4$ cups basic vegetable stock
 (see page 10)
salt and freshly ground black pepper

Trim the celery, wash and thinly slice. Heat
the margarine and the oil in a large saucepan,
add the celery and onion and cover. Simmer
for 10 minutes, shaking the pan until the
vegetables are softened.

Add the apricots, stock and seasonings and
bring to the boil. Cover the pan, reduce the
heat and simmer for 45 minutes.

Allow the soup to cool and transfer to a food
processor. Blend until smooth and return to
the cleaned saucepan. Heat gently until
thoroughly heated through. Ladle into soup
bowls and serve.

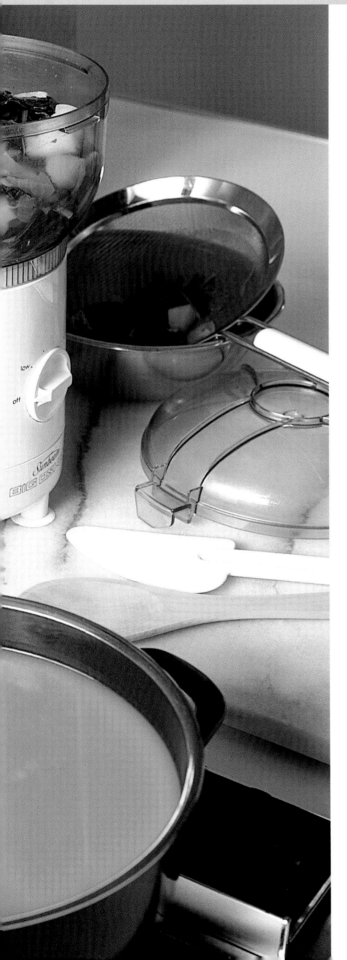

RED PEPPER SOUP

Serves 4

2 tablespoons oil
1 garlic clove
2 red (bell) peppers, diced
1 brown onion, roughly chopped
1 carrot, roughly chopped
2 celery sticks, sliced
1 kg/2^1/$_4$ lb ripe tomatoes, peeled
pinch of saffron or ground turmeric, optional
2 tablespoons short-grain rice
750 ml/1^1/$_4$ pints/3 cups basic chicken stock (see page 9)
1 tablespoon tomato purée (paste)
^{1}/$_2$ teaspoon dried basil
salt and freshly ground black pepper
Garnish
double (heavy) cream, optional
red (bell) pepper, seeded and finely chopped
sprigs of herbs

Heat the oil in a saucepan, add the garlic, peppers and onion and cook for 2 minutes. Add the carrot and celery, tomatoes and saffron or turmeric, if using, and cook for another 2 minutes. Stir in the rice, cover and cook gently for 5 minutes.

Add the stock to the pan, stir in the tomato paste and basil. Cover and simmer over a low heat for 1 hour.

Season with salt and pepper and transfer the soup to a food processor. Blend until smooth and return to the clean saucepan. Reheat, stirring regularly until just boiling.

Adjust the seasonings and serve with the cream, if using, chopped peppers and herbs.

SWEET POTATO AND SPINACH DUO

Serves 6

For the sweet potato soup
675 g/1¹/₂ lb sweet potatoes, coarsely chopped
4 carrots, coarsely chopped
1 litre/1³/₄ pints/4¹/₄ cups basic chicken stock (see page 9)
5 cm/2 inch cinnamon stick
salt and freshly ground black pepper

For the spinach soup
30 g/1 oz/2 tablespoons butter
1 onion, chopped
1 bunch spinach, washed, trimmed and chopped
1 potato, chopped
1 litre/1³/₄ pints/4¹/₄ cups basic chicken stock (see page 9)
2 strips of orange peel, pith removed
salt and freshly ground black pepper
pinch of ground nutmeg

Place the sweet potatoes, carrots, stock and cinnamon stick in a large saucepan. Bring to the boil, then cover. Reduce the heat and simmer for 30 minutes or until the vegetables are tender. Discard the cinnamon stick.

Transfer the soup to a food processor and blend until smooth. Season with salt and pepper and return the purée to a clean saucepan and leave to stand.

Melt the butter for the spinach soup in a large saucepan and cook the onion over a low heat for 5 minutes. Add the spinach, potato, stock and orange peel.

Season with salt, pepper and nutmeg, cover and simmer for 25 minutes. Discard the orange peel and transfer the soup to a food processor. Blend until smooth. Return the soup to a clean saucepan.

Reheat both soups, stirring regularly over a low heat until just boiling. Holding a pan of soup in each hand, or using two ladles, carefully pour the soups together into shallow soup bowls, pouring one soup on each side of the bowl so that they naturally meet in the centre. Serve with bread sticks or small savoury muffins.

PARSLEY AND POTATO SOUP

Serves 4

2 rindless bacon rashers (slices), chopped
30 g/1 oz/2 tablespoons butter
1 potato, diced
1 onion, chopped
500 ml/17 fl oz/2¼ cups basic vegetable stock (see page 10)
3–4 tablespoons milk
salt and freshly ground black pepper
3 tablespoons freshly chopped parsley
4 tablespoons single (light) cream
garlic croûtons to serve (see page 147)

Dry-fry the bacon in a large saucepan, until the fat begins to run. Add the butter, potato and onion and fry for 2–3 minutes until softened.

Add the stock and milk and bring to the boil. Reduce the heat, cover and simmer for 25 minutes until the vegetables are tender.

Transfer the soup to a food processor and blend until smooth. Return the soup to the clean pan, season with salt and pepper and add the parsley and cream. Reheat gently without boiling and serve with garlic croûtons.

RED APPLE SOUP

Serves 4

4 tablespoons clear honey
pinch of salt
600 ml/1 pint/2½ cups basic vegetable stock (see page 10)
1.5 kg/3¼ lb red dessert apples, peeled, cored and chopped
60 g/2 oz/1 cup brown bread crumbs
1 teaspoon ground cinnamon
zest of 1 lemon
400 ml/14 fl oz/1¾ cups red wine
2 tablespoons low-sugar raspberry jam
4 tablespoons natural yogurt

Place the honey, salt and stock in a saucepan and bring to the boil. Add the apples, bread crumbs, cinnamon and lemon zest, reduce the heat and simmer for 10 minutes until the apples have softened. Transfer the mixture to a food processor and blend until smooth.

Return the mixture to a clean saucepan and add the wine and jam, simmer gently, stirring until the jam has dissolved.

Ladle the soup into warmed serving bowls and swirl the yogurt into the top of each portion. Serve immediately.

CARROT AND ORANGE SOUP

Serves 4-6

2 tablespoons olive oil
675 g/1¹/₂ lb carrots, sliced
1 leek, sliced
1 litre/1³/₄ pints/4¹/₄ cups basic chicken stock (see page 9)
1 large orange

Heat the oil in a saucepan and sauté the carrots and leek for 10 minutes until softened but not browned.

Add the stock and bring to the boil. Reduce the heat and simmer for 40 minutes, or until the vegetables are tender. Transfer the mixture to a food processor and blend until smooth.

Return the mixture to a clean saucepan and add the stock. Meanwhile, pare half of the orange rind, cut into narrow strips and cook in a separate saucepan in boiling water until tender.

Grate the remaining orange rind into the soup and squeeze the juice from the orange into the soup. Strain the orange rind and use to garnish the soup. Serve immediately.

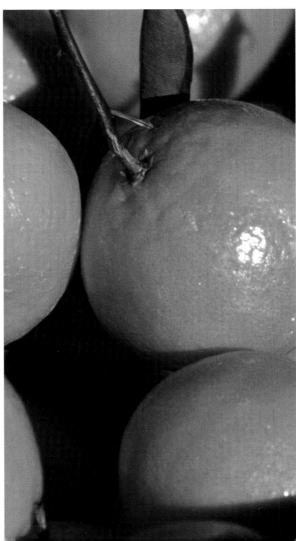

WATERCRESS SOUP

Serves 4

450 g/1 lb potatoes
1 garlic clove, crushed
1 shallot, chopped
1.25 litres/2¼ pints/5¾ cups basic vegetable stock
 (see page 10)
salt and freshly ground black pepper
30 g/1 oz/2 tablespoons butter
30 g/1 oz/¼ cup plain (all-purpose) flour
2 bunches watercress, finely chopped
croûtons to serve (see page 147)

Place the potatoes, garlic and shallot in a large saucepan with the stock. Season well, bring to the boil and then simmer for 15 minutes. Drain and reserve the liquid, and purée the vegetables in a food processor.

Melt the butter in a large saucepan and add the flour. Mix well and cook for 1 minute. Add the potato stock and the puréed vegetables and bring to the boil. Cover and simmer for 30 minutes.

Add the watercress and simmer for 5 minutes. Serve immediately with croûtons.

HOT BEAN SOUP

Serves 4

1 onion
2 carrots
1 teaspoon olive oil
2 garlic cloves, crushed
$^1/_2$ teaspoon chilli powder
$^1/_2$ teaspoon garam masala
400 g/14 oz can red kidney beans in salted water,
 drained and rinsed
2 tablespoons tomato purée
600 ml/1 pint/2$^1/_2$ cups basic chicken stock
salt and freshly ground black pepper
2 tablespoons freshly chopped coriander (cilantro)

Peel and chop the onion and carrots. Heat the oil in a large saucepan and sauté the onion, carrots and garlic for 5 minutes, stirring until lightly browned.

Add the spices and cook for 1 minute. Add the drained beans, tomato purée, stock and seasoning. Bring to the boil.

Reduce the heat and simmer for 30 minutes until the vegetables are tender.

Transfer half of the soup to a food processor and blend until smooth. Return to the pan and mix well. Heat through and serve.

SPINACH AND POTATO SOUP

Serves 4

1 red onion
225 g/8 oz potatoes
1 teaspoon olive oil
2 garlic cloves, crushed
400 ml/14 fl oz/1³/₄ cups basic vegetable stock (see page 10)
pinch of ground cinnamon
120 g/4 oz baby spinach, trimmed
125 ml/4 fl oz/¹/₂ cup yogurt

Peel and chop the onion and potatoes. Heat the oil in a saucepan and sauté the vegetables with the garlic for 5 minutes, stirring until lightly browned.

Add the stock and cinnamon and bring to the boil. Cover and simmer for 15 minutes.

Wash the spinach, drain and shake off any excess water. Add the spinach to the soup, cover and cook for another 5 minutes.

Transfer the soup to a food processor and blend until smooth. Add the yogurt and return to the pan to heat through. Do not allow to boil. Ladle into serving bowls and serve with garlic croûtons (see page 147).

CURRIED POTATO SOUP

Serves 4

60 g/2 oz/¹/₄ cup butter
4 medium-sized potatoes, diced
2 garlic clove, crushed
2 red eating apples, peeled, cored and chopped
2 teaspoons mild curry powder
¹/₂ teaspoon mild chilli powder
1.15 litres/2 pints/5 cups basic chicken stock (see page 9)
150 ml/¹/₄ pint/²/₃ cup yogurt
freshly chopped coriander (cilantro) to garnish

Melt the butter in a large saucepan and sauté the potatoes, garlic and apples for 10 minutes, stirring frequently.

Add the curry and chilli powders and fry for 1–2 minutes. Pour in the stock and bring to the boil. Reduce the heat and cover, and simmer for 25 minutes until the vegetables are tender.

Transfer the soup to a food processor and blend until smooth. Return the soup to the cleaned saucepan and stir in the yogurt.

Ladle the soup into serving bowls and garnish with chopped coriander.

ORANGE AND WATERCRESS SOUP

<u>Serves 6</u>

2 bunches watercress

4 tablespoons olive oil

1 leek, sliced

1 garlic clove, crushed

3 tablespoons plain (all-purpose) flour

1.15 litres/2 pints/5 cups basic chicken stock (see page 9)

finely grated rind of 1 orange

juice of 1 orange

orange slices and watercress leaves to garnish

Trim and rinse the watercress and chop finely. Heat the oil in a large saucepan and sauté the leek and garlic for 5 minutes until softened. Add the chopped watercress and cook gently for another 5 minutes.

Remove the pan from the heat and stir in the flour and stock. Return the pan to the heat, cover and simmer for 30 minutes until the vegetables are tender.

Stir in the orange rind and juice and transfer the soup to a food processor. Blend until smooth. Return the soup to the cleaned pan and reheat gently. Garnish and serve immediately.

Cold soups are coming into their own in the culinary world and are increasingly popular. Perfect on a hot day for picnics, as a starter at a barbecue or for an elegant outdoor supper, they use ingredients such as cucumber, melon and cooked vegetables both bright and subtle in colour. Some soups are specifically designed to be served cold and others may be served either hot or cold, such as vichyssoise. All cold soups should be served well chilled, and a few ice cubes added before serving is the ideal way to keep them cool when time is short.

VICHYSSOISE

Serves 6

4 leeks, washed and sliced

4 potatoes, chopped

1.8 litres/3 pints/2 quarts basic chicken stock (see page 9)

30 g/1 oz/2 tablespoons butter

pinch of paprika

$^1/_2$ teaspoon ground black pepper

pinch of cayenne pepper

250 ml/8 fl oz/1 cup milk

125 ml/4 fl oz/$^1/_2$ cup single (light) cream

freshly snipped chives to garnish

In a large saucepan sauté the leeks and potatoes in the butter. Add the chicken stock and spices and simmer for 40 minutes or until the vegetables are tender.

Transfer to a food processor and blend until smooth. Return to the cleaned saucepan and add the milk and cream. Simmer gently, but do not allow to boil.

Place in a large serving bowl or soup tureen, cover and chill for 3 hours. Sprinkle with snipped chives and serve.

CUCUMBER SOUP

Serves 6

375 g/13 oz/3 cups cucumber, peeled and chopped
1 onion, chopped
750 ml/1¼ pints/3 cups basic chicken stock (see page 9)
bouquet garni (to include dill and lemon peel)
salt and freshly ground black pepper
250 ml/8 fl oz/1 cup natural yogurt or soured cream
30 g/1 oz/½ cup freshly chopped dill
2 spring onions (scallions), finely chopped

Place half of the cucumber and the onion in a large saucepan with the chicken stock, bouquet garni, salt and pepper. Bring to the boil, reduce the heat and simmer for 15 minutes.

Remove the bouquet garni and transfer the soup to a food processor. Blend until smooth and transfer to a soup tureen. Leave to cool.

Place the remainder of the cucumber in the food processor with the yogurt or soured cream and blend until smooth. Add to the soup in the tureen and stir in the dill and spring onions. Chill in the refrigerator until ready to serve.

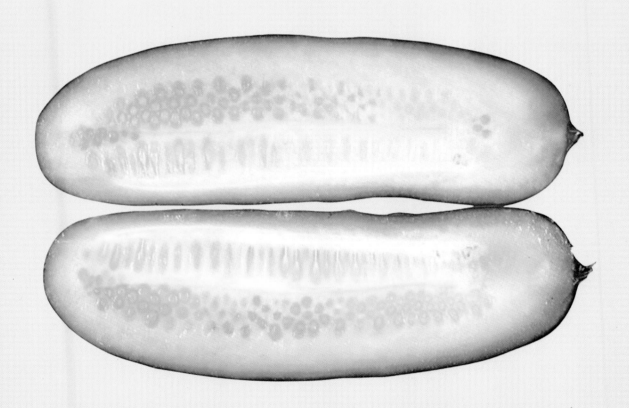

AUBERGINE AND YOGURT SOUP

Serves 4-6

6 medium-sized aubergines (egg plants)
3–4 tablespoons oil
3 green (bell) peppers, skinned, seeded and chopped
675 ml/22 fl oz/2³/₄ cups natural yogurt
1 teaspoon salt
¹/₂ teaspoon freshly ground black pepper
large pinch cayenne pepper
2 garlic cloves, crushed
1 tablespoon freshly chopped mint

Remove the dark skin from the aubergines and cut the flesh in half lengthways. Sprinkle salt over the cut surfaces and set aside, cut side uppermost, for 30 minutes to sweat. Wipe dry with paper towels and gently squeeze to remove the bitter juices.

Heat the oil in a large saucepan and sauté the aubergines and green peppers, without browning, until tender.

Transfer to a food processor and blend until smooth. Pour into a soup tureen and stir in the yogurt. Add the remaining ingredients and chill in the refrigerator until ready to serve. This soup should be served ice cold.

GAZPACHO

Serves 8

1.5 kg/3¼ lb ripe tomatoes
3 shallots
2 cucumbers
5 tablespoons oil
5 tablespoons lemon juice
salt and freshly ground black pepper
Tabasco sauce to taste
1 Spanish red onion, chopped
2 green (bell) peppers
toasted seasoned croûtons to garnish (see page 147)

Blanch the tomatoes in hot water for 5 minutes. Peel and core them and cut into chunks. Place the tomatoes in a food processor and purée in batches.

Peel the shallots and add to the last batch of tomatoes in the food processor. Sieve the tomato mixture into a large bowl to remove the seeds.

Peel one of the cucumbers, halve lengthways and remove any seeds with a teaspoon. Cut into small pieces and blend in a food processor, adding the oil and lemon juice while processing. Add this mixture to the tomatoes, season and add a few drops of Tabasco sauce. Mix well, cover and refrigerate for several hours.

Peel and chop the onion and set aside. Peel the second cucumber, halve lengthways and remove any seeds. Dice the cucumber and refrigerate with the onion.

Put the green peppers under the grill (broiler) to char the skin. Remove and peel off the skin. Remove the stems and seeds and chop the flesh into small dice. Refrigerate.

When ready to serve the gazpacho, mix all of the prepared vegetables together. Add a few ice cubes to the soup and serve in individual bowls, garnished with croûtons.

PLUM SOUP

Serves 8

2 tablespoons fine tapioca
1.5 litres/2³/₄ pints/7 cups basic chicken stock (see page 9)
1 kg/2¹/₄ lb plums, washed and stemmed
500 ml/17 fl oz/2 cups sweet white wine
90 g/3 oz/¹/₃ cup caster (superfine) sugar
2 chillis
2 whole cloves
1 lemon, finely sliced
1 teaspoon salt
1 teaspoon ground nutmeg
4 lemon slices

Dissolve the tapioca by bringing 500 ml/ 17 fl oz/2 cups of the stock to the boil, reducing to a simmer and then gradually adding the tapioca. Stirring constantly, continue to simmer until it is translucent.

Put the plums into a large saucepan with the rest of the stock, the wine, sugar, chillis, cloves and lemon. Bring to the boil and simmer until the plums are tender. Remove the plums, lemon slices and chillis.

Skin the plums and cut in half to remove the stones (pits). Return the plums to the soup and add the salt and nutmeg.

Stir the tapioca mixture into the soup and chill in the refrigerator until ready to serve. Serve chilled with half a lemon slice to garnish each bowl.

SUMMER SWEET PEPPER SOUP

Serves 4

4 tablespoons freshly chopped coriander (cilantro)
2 sweet red (bell) peppers
I small onion, sliced
175 g/6 oz/I cup ripe tomatoes, sliced
I litre/I³/₄ pints/4¹/₄ cups basic vegetable stock
 (see page 10)
150 ml/¹/₄ pint/²/₃ cup milk
¹/₂ teaspoon salt
freshly ground black pepper

Spread the chopped coriander across an ice-cube tray and add water. Freeze until solid.

Cut the stems from the red (bell) peppers, remove the seeds and slice the flesh into strips.

In a large saucepan, combine the peppers, onion, tomatoes and stock. Bring to the boil, lower the heat, cover and simmer until all the vegetables are tender, about 15 minutes.

Drain the liquid into a separate pot and purée the vegetables in a food processor. Then combine the liquid and purée, add the milk and season to taste.

Refrigerate for at least 3 hours. Add the ice-cubes to the soup bowls when ready to serve.

ICED LEMON SOUP

Serves 4

finely grated rind of ¹/₂ lemon
4 egg yolks
juice of 2 lemons
3–4 tablespoons soured cream
350 ml/12 fl oz/1¹/₂ cups basic chicken stock (see page 9)
3–4 tablespoons single (light) cream
snipped chives to garnish

Combine the lemon rind with the egg yolks and beat well. Blend in the lemon juice and the soured cream.

Heat the stock and gradually add to the egg yolk mixture, stirring constantly. Cook over a very low heat and stir until the mixture thickens to a thin custard consistency. Remove from the heat, season with salt and pepper and leave to cool, stirring occasionally.

Chill thoroughly and serve garnished with snipped chives.

BORSCH

Serves 4

750 g/1³/₄ lb fresh beetroot
1 large onion, finely chopped
1 celery stick, finely chopped
¹/₂ carrot, coarsely grated
400 ml/14 fl oz/1³/₄ cups canned beef consommé or
 beef stock (see page 8)
1 stalk of parsley
1 sprig dill
3 cloves
sugar, salt and freshly ground black pepper
2–3 tablespoons lemon juice
Garnish
soured cream or natural yogurt
spring onions (scallions) or chives, finely snipped
black and red caviar

Peel and coarsely grate two of the beetroots. Place the grated beetroot in a saucepan with the other vegetables and add the beef consommé, made up as directed on the can, or the fresh stock. Stir in the parsley, dill and cloves. Bring to the boil, reduce the heat and simmer for 30 minutes.

Strain through a fine sieve and discard the solids. Stir in some sugar and lemon juice to taste. Season with salt and pepper.

Peel and coarsely grate the remaining beetroot, and add it to the soup. Chill thoroughly. Serve with a spoonful of soured cream or yogurt, a sprinkling of spring onions or chives and the caviar.

GUACAMOLE CHILL

Serves 6

2 large, ripe avocados
500 ml/17 fl oz/2¼ cups buttermilk
500 ml/17 fl oz/2¼ cups basic chicken stock (see page 9)
2 tablespoons lemon juice
2 tablespoons freshly chopped coriander (cilantro)
 or 2 teaspoons ground coriander
1–2 tablespoons mild chilli sauce
Garnish
1 small white onion, finely chopped
1 tomato, peeled and finely chopped
coriander (cilantro) leaves

Cut one of the avocados in half, remove the stone (pit), peel off the skin and chop the flesh roughly. Place in a food processor and blend to a creamy purée. Add the buttermilk and chicken stock and blend again to combine. Stir in the lemon juice and coriander.

Pour the soup into a bowl, season with the chilli sauce and cover tightly with cling film (plastic wrap) to exclude the air. Chill for at least 1 hour.

Stone the remaining avocado, peel and chop the flesh into small dice. Stir into the soup and adjust the seasoning.

Serve with a spoonful of the onion and tomato on top with a sprinkling of chopped coriander.

ICED CURRY FRUITS

Serves 6

2 cooking apples, cored and roughly chopped
1 banana, chopped
125 g/4 oz/1 cup pawpaw (papaya), peeled,
 seeded and chopped
4 spring onions (scallions), finely chopped
400 ml/14 fl oz/1³/₄ cups tomato juice
250 ml/8 fl oz/1 cup basic chicken stock (see page 9)
¹/₂ teaspoon curry powder
salt and freshly ground black pepper
250 ml/8 fl oz/1 cup double (heavy) cream
3 tablespoons desiccated (shredded) coconut
1 cooking apple, peeled and coarsely grated or chopped
cooked strips of poppadum (see page 148) to garnish

Place the cooking apples, banana, pawpaw and
spring onions in a food processor and blend
until smooth. Blend in the tomato juice, stock
and curry powder.

Pour into a large bowl, adjust the seasonings
and leave to chill for several hours.

Place the cream in a bowl and whip until it
forms soft peaks. Fold in the coconut and
grated or chopped apple and leave to chill.

Serve the soup with a spoonful of the cream
mixture and poppadum strips.

ICED CUCUMBER AND MINT SOUP

Serves 4-6

1 large, unpeeled cucumber
250 ml/8 fl oz/1 cup natural yogurt
1 small green (bell) pepper, seeded and finely chopped
1 garlic clove, crushed
2 tablespoons wine vinegar
2 tablespoons freshly chopped mint
salt and freshly ground black pepper
250 ml/8 fl oz/1 cup milk
mint leaves to garnish

Grate the cucumber into a bowl and stir in the yogurt, green pepper, garlic, wine vinegar and mint.

Season well to taste, cover and chill for at least 2 hours.

Just before serving, stir in the milk and garnish with mint leaves. Serve immediately.

AVOCADO SOUP

Serves 6

2 ripe avocados
1 red onion, chopped
grated rind and juice of 1 lime
250 ml/8 fl oz/1 cup natural yogurt
500 ml/17 fl oz/2^1/$_4$ cups chilled basic chicken stock
 (see page 9)
salt and cayenne pepper
chopped tomatoes or croutons to garnish

Halve the avocados and remove the stones (pits).
Scoop the flesh out with a teaspoon.

Place the avocado flesh, onion, lime rind and
juice, and yogurt in a food processor and
blend until smooth.

Turn out into a large serving bowl and whisk
in the stock. Season and cover tightly. Chill for
at least 1 hour. Garnish and serve at once.

SUMMER SOUP

Serves 4-6

3 tablespoons olive oil
1 onion, chopped
2 garlic cloves, crushed
2 green (bell) peppers, seeded and chopped
450 g/1lb ripe tomatoes, chopped
900 ml/1½ pints/3¾ cups basic vegetable stock
  (see page 10)
1 tablespoon red wine vinegar
pinch of chilli powder
freshly ground black pepper
4 tablespoons mayonnaise or natural yogurt

Heat the oil in a large saucepan and sauté the onion and garlic for 5 minutes until softened.

Add the green peppers and cook for another 5 minutes, stirring occasionally. Add the tomatoes and stir to break them up. Pour in the stock, cover and simmer the soup for 50 minutes.

Transfer the soup to a food processor and blend until smooth. Pass through a sieve to remove the tomato skins.

Place the mayonnaise or yogurt in a bowl and gradually whisk in the soup. Cover and chill in the refrigerator for 3 hours. Serve chilled with ice cubes.

CHILLED FENNEL SOUP

Serves 4

450 g/1 lb fennel bulbs
30 g/1 oz/2 tablespoons butter
1 onion, chopped
750 ml/1 1/4 pints/3 cups basic chicken stock (see page 9)
salt and freshly ground black pepper
150 ml/1/4 pint/2/3 cup soured cream
celery leaves to garnish

Remove the green leaves from the fennel. Peel and discard the outer layers from the bulbs and chop the bulbs roughly.

Melt the butter in a large saucepan, add the fennel and onions and sauté for 10 minutes, stirring frequently.

Pour in the stock, season and bring to the boil. Reduce the heat to a simmer, cover and cook for 20 minutes until the fennel is tender.

Transfer the soup to a food processor and blend until smooth. Beat in the soured cream and place in a bowl. Cover and chill overnight before serving, garnished with celery leaves.

CHILLED APPLE SOUP

Serves 4

2 teaspoons butter
2 teaspoons plain (all-purpose) flour
I tablespoon medium curry powder
pinch of chilli powder
750 ml/1¼ pints/3 cups basic chicken stock (see page 9)
salt and freshly ground black pepper
200 ml/7 fl oz/¾ cup single (light) cream
I dessert apple
juice of I small lime
mint sprigs to garnish

Melt the butter in a large saucepan and add the flour, curry powder and chilli powder. Stir well and cook for 1 minute.

Gradually stir in the stock and bring to the boil. Remove from the heat and season. Cover for 3 hours and chill the soup.

Whisk the cream into the soup. Peel and grate the apple and toss in the lime juice.

Mix the apple into the soup and ladle into serving bowls. Garnish with mint and serve immediately.

SPANISH CHILLED SOUP

Serves 4

750 g/1³/₄ lb ripe tomatoes
10cm/4 inch piece of dry French bread
4 tablespoons sherry vinegar
2 garlic cloves, crushed
125 ml/4 fl oz/¹/₂ cup olive oil
1 egg yolk
1 tablespoon freshly chopped basil

Peel and seed the tomatoes. Chop the flesh. Soak the bread in the vinegar and place in a food processor with the tomatoes, garlic, oil and egg yolk. Blend until smooth.

Transfer the soup to a serving bowl and chill for 3 hours.

Garnish with basil and serve immediately.

CHILLED ALMOND SOUP

Serves 4

3–4 slices stale bread
475 ml/16 fl oz/2 cups basic chicken stock (see page 9)
125 g/4 oz/1 cup blanched almonds
3 garlic cloves
150 ml/¹/₄ pint/²/₃ cup olive oil
3 tablespoons garlic vinegar
1 tablespoon sherry

Soak the bread in the stock and then place in a food processor with the almonds and garlic and blend until smooth.

Gradually beat in the oil and vinegar. Stir in the sherry.

Transfer to a serving dish and chill for 3 hours before serving.

CHERRY SOUP

Serves 4

350 g/12 oz/3 cups black cherries
250 ml/8 fl oz/1 cup dry red wine
juice of 1 orange
1 tablespoon caster (superfine) sugar
1 tablespoon brandy
fresh cherries and mint sprigs to garnish

Remove the stalks and stones (pits) from the cherries. Place the cherries in a saucepan with the wine, orange juice and sugar. Bring to the boil and then simmer for 5 minutes.

Blend the cherries with the cooking liquid in a food processor until smooth.

Transfer to a serving dish and stir in the brandy. Cover and chill for 3 hours.

Ladle into serving bowls and garnish with fresh cherries and mint. Serve immediately.

COLD SOUPS

CITRUS ALMOND SOUP

<u>Serves 6</u>

30 g/1 oz/2 tablespoons butter
1 onion, chopped
2 garlic cloves, crushed
30 g/1 oz/^{1}/$_4$ cup plain (all-purpose) flour
750 ml/1^1/$_4$ pints/3 cups basic chicken stock (see page 9)
grated rind and juice of 1 small lemon
grated rind and juice of 1 small lime
salt and freshly ground black pepper
250 ml/8 fl oz/1 cup single (light) cream
60 g/2 oz/^{1}/$_2$ cup flaked almonds, toasted
citrus zest to garnish

Melt the butter in a saucepan and fry the onion and garlic for 3–4 minutes, stirring. Stir in the flour and cook for 1 minute.

Gradually add the stock and bring to the boil. Add the lemon and lime rind and juice and season to taste.

Cover and simmer for 20 minutes.

Allow the soup to cool a little, then transfer to a food processor and blend until smooth. Stir in the cream and chop the almonds. Stir into the soup.

Cover and chill the soup for 3 hours, ladle into soup bowls and garnish with citrus zest.

GARLIC SOUP

Serves 6

500 ml/17 fl oz/2¼ cups basic chicken stock (see page 9)
1.5 litres/2¾ pints/7 cups water
a bouquet garni
30 g/1 oz/2 tablespoons goose fat or butter
24 garlic cloves, peeled
salt and freshly ground black pepper
1 teaspoon grated nutmeg
3 eggs, separated
6 slices stale bread
2 tablespoons olive oil

Bring the stock to the boil in a large saucepan with the water and bouquet garni. Remove from the heat. Melt the goose fat or butter in a separate, large saucepan and add the garlic. Cook gently and just before the garlic browns, pour the stock over the top. Add the salt, pepper and nutmeg and cook for 15 minutes. Blend the mixture in a food processor and return to the cleaned saucepan.

Spread the egg whites on to the stale bread and toast in a preheated oven at 180°C/350°F/Gas 4 until they crispen.

Beat the egg yolks and olive oil together and add a little of the soup mixture to the egg yolks. Gradually pour the mixture into the soup, stirring. Do not let the soup return to the boil, otherwise the eggs will curdle.

To serve the soup, place a slice of toasted bread in the base of each bowl and ladle the soup over the top.

Gumbos are the trade mark of Cajun cooking, and are basically very thick soups or stews and are really meals in themselves. Gumbo is so called because of the African word for okra 'gumbo', but it is a misconception that okra is a vital ingredient. Usually served with, or over, rice, the recipes all taste very individual and are full of flavour.

A bisque is a creamy purée that concentrates the inclusion of one main ingredient into a rich, filling soup. Fish and shellfish are most frequently used, but meat and poultry or vegetables work just as well. The main ingredient is usually sautéed and then flambéed in a spirit, usually brandy, the resultant soup being puréed to give a creamy texture.

A chowder is a thick and substantial soup, originating in North America. The name comes from the French for stew pot 'chaudière'. The ingredients may be varied, but again fish and shellfish chowders are most commonly found. With gumbos and chowders, it is recommended they be prepared the day before eating, to allow the flavours to develop fully.

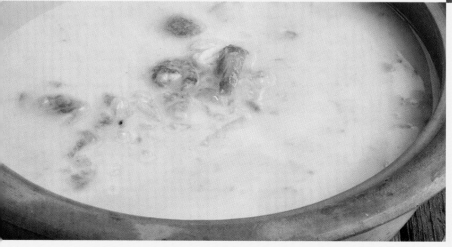

SMOKED FISH CHOWDER

Serves 4

450 g/1 lb smoked fish fillet, such as haddock or cod
1.25 litres/2¼ pints/5¾ cups basic fish stock (see page 9)
60 g/2 oz/¼ cup butter
1 leek, sliced
2 tablespoons plain (all-purpose) flour
225 g/8 oz potatoes, cut into dice
2 carrots, grated
150 ml/¼ pint/⅔ cup single (light) cream
freshly chopped dill to garnish

Place the fish in a saucepan with the stock and cook for 10 minutes. Drain, reserving the stock, and flake the fish.

Melt the butter in a large saucepan and sauté the leek for 2–3 minutes until softened. Stir in the flour and cook for 1 minute. Gradually add the stock and bring to the boil, stirring. Add the potatoes and carrots and cook for another 10 minutes.

Stir in the cream and flaked fish. Season to taste and heat through, but do not allow to boil. Sprinkle with chopped dill and serve immediately.

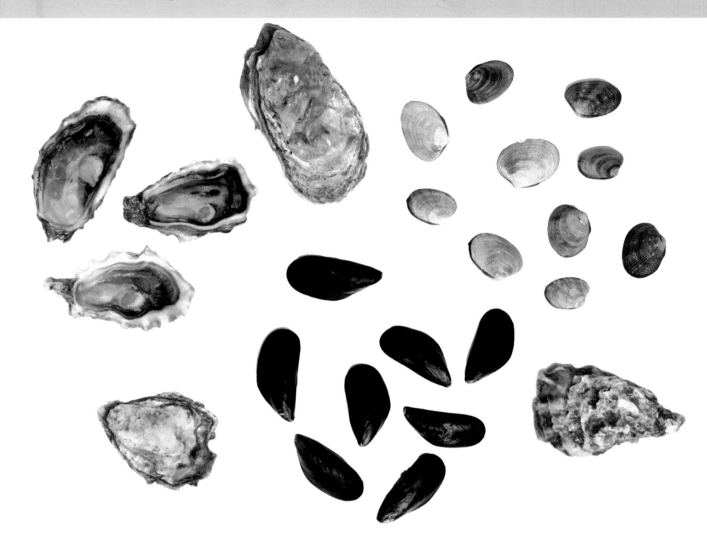

BOUILLABAISSE

Serves 6

900 g/2 lb mixed white fish, skinned, and shellfish
150 ml/¼ pint/⅔ cup olive oil
2 onions, sliced
1 garlic clove, crushed
1 celery stick, sliced
250 g/9 oz/1¼ cups tomatoes, skinned and chopped
1 bay leaf
pinch of saffron
freshly snipped chives to garnish

Cut the fish into large chunks. Heat the oil in a heavy-based saucepan and fry the onions for 5 minutes, until softened but not browned.

Add the garlic, celery, tomatoes and herbs. Dissolve the saffron in 2 tablespoons hot water.

Combine the fish and vegetables and stir in the herbs. Add enough cold water to cover and stir in the saffron water. Bring to the boil and simmer for 8 minutes.

Add the shellfish and cook for another 7–8 minutes until cooked through. Garnish with chives and serve.

PRAWN SOUP

Serves 4

250 g/9 oz large prawns (shrimp) in their shell,
 either raw or cooked
300 ml/¹/₂ pint/1¹/₄ cups basic fish stock (see page 9)
2 tablespoons olive oil
1 onion, chopped
1 carrot, chopped
2 tablespoons plain (all-purpose) flour
1 tablespoon tomato purée
3 tablespoons Madeira
150 ml/¹/₄ pint/²/₃ cup single (light) cream

Shell the prawns and boil the shells in the stock for 5 minutes. Strain the liquid, discarding the shells.

Heat the oil in a large saucepan and fry the onion and carrot for 5 minutes until softened. Add the flour and cook for 1 minute. Stir in the stock and tomato purée. Boil for 10 minutes, then transfer to a food processor and blend until smooth.

Add the shelled prawns and Madeira and boil for 5 minutes. Blend the cream into the soup and season to taste.

SWEETCORN AND PRAWN CHOWDER

Serves 4

1 leek, chopped
1 tablespoon butter
450 g/1 lb potatoes
300 ml/^{1}/$_2$ pint/1^1/$_4$ cups basic fish stock (see page 9)
200 g/7 oz/1^1/$_2$ cups peeled prawns (shrimp)
175 g/6 oz/^{3}/$_4$ cup sweetcorn
600 ml/1 pint/2^1/$_2$ cups milk
60 g/2 oz/^{1}/$_2$ cup strong Cheddar cheese, grated

Cook the leek in the butter in a large saucepan for 3–4 minutes. Add the potatoes and stock and bring to the boil.

Reduce the heat and simmer for 10–15 minutes until the potatoes are cooked.

Stir in the prawns, sweetcorn and milk and heat through thoroughly. Sprinkle the cheese on top and serve immediately.

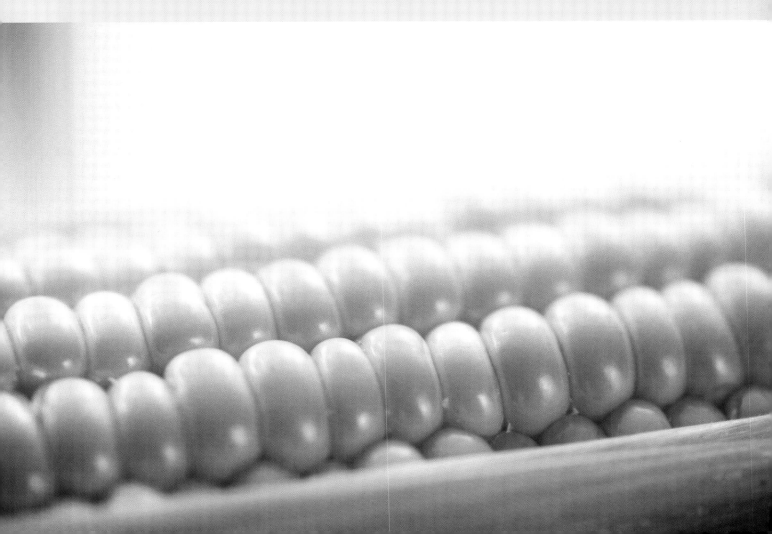

SWEETCORN AND HAM CHOWDER

Serves 4

2 tablespoons butter

1 red onion, finely chopped

3 tablespoons plain (all-purpose) flour

90 g/3 oz/¹/₃ cup cream cheese

300 ml/¹/₂ pint/1¹/₄ cups basic fish stock (see page 9)

150 ml/¹/₄ pint/²/₃ cup milk

400 g/14 oz can sweetcorn, drained

150 ml/¹/₄ pint/²/₃ cup double (thick) cream

150 g/5 oz/1 cup smoked ham, chopped

Melt the butter in a large saucepan and sauté the onion for 2–3 minutes. Stir in the flour and cook for 1 minute. Add the cream cheese and whisk in the stock and milk.

Add the corn and simmer for 10 minutes.

Stir in the cream and ham and heat through thoroughly. Serve hot.

PRAWN BISQUE

Serves 4

300 ml/¹/₂ pint/1¹/₄ cups basic fish stock (see page 9)
300 ml/¹/₂ pint/1¹/₄ cups milk
450 g/1 lb uncooked prawns (shrimp)
1 tablespoon short-grain rice
1 bay leaf
1 tablespoon freshly chopped dill
300 ml/¹/₂ pint/1¹/₄ cups dry white wine
pinch of turmeric
600 ml/1 pint/2¹/₂ cups single (light) cream
dill sprigs to garnish

Mix the stock and milk in a large saucepan and bring to the boil. Cook the prawns in the liquid for 2 minutes, and remove with a draining spoon. Set aside.

Strain the liquid into another saucepan. Add the rice, bay leaf and dill and cook while shelling the prawns, leaving a few for garnish.

After 30 minutes the rice will be broken down and the liquid thickened. Place the shelled prawns in a food processor with a little of the liquid and blend until smooth. Return to the pan, add the wine and simmer for 7–8 minutes.

Add the turmeric. Blend the reserved unshelled prawns in a food processor with half of the cream and press through a sieve into the soup. Stir in the remaining cream and top with herbs. Serve immediately.

CRAB BISQUE

Serves 4

1 medium-sized cooked crab
60 g/2 oz/$^1/_3$ cup long-grain rice
600 ml/1 pint/2$^1/_2$ cups milk
30 g/1 oz/2 tablespoons butter
pinch ground nutmeg
600 ml/1 pint/2$^1/_2$ cups basic fish stock (see page 9)
few drops of anchovy essence (extract)
150 ml/$^1/_4$ pint/$^2/_3$ cup single (light) cream
cayenne pepper
freshly snipped chives to garnish

Place the rice, milk and butter in a saucepan with the nutmeg and bring to the boil. Reduce the heat and simmer until the rice is tender.

Add the brown crabmeat and blend in a food processor. Return to the pan and add the stock, anchovy essence and white crabmeat.

Stir in the cream and add cayenne pepper to taste. Heat through without allowing the bisque to boil and garnish with chives.

CORN AND BACON CHOWDER

Serves 6

15 g/¹/₂ oz/1 tablespoon butter
4 bacon rashers (slices), rind and fat removed, chopped
1 onion, thinly sliced
500 g/18 oz potatoes, cut into 2.5 cm/1 inch cubes
1 litre/1³/₄ pints/4¹/₄ cups boiling water
400 g/14 oz can sweetcorn kernels or creamed sweetcorn
400 ml/14 fl oz/1³/₄ cups milk
¹/₂ teaspoon dried thyme
salt and freshly ground black pepper
Worcestershire sauce

Melt the butter in a large saucepan. Add the chopped bacon and the onion and sauté until the onion is soft and the bacon slightly crisp. Add the potatoes and water and simmer, uncovered, for 10–15 minutes until the potatoes are tender but not mushy.

Stir in the sweetcorn, milk and thyme and bring the soup to the boil.

Season with salt and pepper and Worcestershire sauce to taste. Ladle into soup bowls and serve.

Variation

Omit the bacon and add 250 g/9 oz/1¹/₄ cups of canned, drained crab meat and 250 g/9 oz/1¹/₂ cups of chopped, shelled prawns (shrimp) or flaked, smoked cod or haddock, with the milk. To prepare the white fish, if using, place in a frying pan (skillet) and cover with water. Simmer for 10–15 minutes until cooked through, remove any skin and bones and flake the fish.

SEAFOOD STEW

Serves 8

2 tablespoons oil
2 leeks, white section only, thinly sliced
2–3 garlic cloves, crushed
2 litres/3^1/$_2$ pints/2^1/$_4$ quarts basic fish stock (see page 9)
400 g/14 oz can whole, peeled tomatoes
1 teaspoon dried thyme
2 teaspoons paprika
1 teaspoon sweet chilli sauce
1 tablespoon tomato purée (paste)
1 kg/2^1/$_4$ lb firm white fish fillets such as cod or haddock,
 cut into large pieces
500 g/18 oz/3 cups green prawns (shrimp), shelled
750 g/1^3/$_4$ lb mussels, scrubbed
250 g/9 oz scallops, washed and trimmed
salt and freshly ground black pepper
freshly chopped parsley and snipped chives to garnish

Heat the oil in a large saucepan. Add the leeks and garlic and sauté over a low heat for 5 minutes. Add the fish stock, tomatoes, thyme, paprika, chilli sauce and tomato purée. Bring the mixture to the boil.

Reduce the heat to a simmer and cook for another 10 minutes. Add the fish, prawns and mussels. Cover and simmer gently until the fish becomes firm and the mussels open. Remove any unopened mussels and discard.

Add the scallops and cook for 2–3 minutes only. Season well with salt and pepper.

Arrange some of the fish in the base of serving bowls and ladle the hot stock over the top. Sprinkle with herbs and serve with garlic bread (see page 155).

SIMPLE SEAFOOD BISQUE

Serves 4-6

450 g/1 lb ripe tomatoes, peeled and chopped
2 brown onions, diced
1.15 litres/2 pints/5 cups cold water
1 teaspoon lemon juice
salt and freshly ground black pepper
450 g/1 lb white fish fillets, cut into cubes
150 ml/¼ pint/⅔ cup light (single) cream
2 tablespoons freshly chopped dill
125 g/4 oz/⅔ cup small cooked prawns (shrimp), shelled

In a large saucepan, mix the tomatoes, onions, water and lemon juice. Season well and bring to the boil. Reduce the heat and simmer for 20 minutes, until the vegetables are tender.

Add the white fish cubes to the soup and cook until just tender, but not falling apart, about 8 minutes.

Stir in the cream and adjust the seasoning to taste. Add the dill and prawns and serve immediately.

CLAM CHOWDER

Serves 4

20 clams
750 ml/1¼ pints/3 cups basic fish stock (see page 9)
300 ml/½ pint/1¼ cups milk
450 g/1 lb potatoes, chopped
30 g/1 oz/2 tablespoons butter
30 g/1 oz/¼ cup flour
salt and freshly ground black pepper
freshly snipped chives to garnish

Boil the clams in a saucepan with enough stock to prevent them burning. Remove the clams from the pan with a slotted draining spoon and remove the meat from the shells.

Chop the meat finely and strain the liquid. Add the remaining stock and pour back into the pan. Add the milk and potatoes and return to the boil. Reduce the heat and simmer for 15 minutes or until the potatoes are tender.

Add the clams and butter and cook for another 10 minutes.

Blend the flour with a little milk to form a paste and blend into the soup until it thickens. Season to taste and garnish with chives. Serve immediately.

BACON AND POTATO CHOWDER

<u>Serves 4</u>

450 g/1 lb potatoes, sliced
30 g/1 oz/2 tablespoons butter
4 rashers (slices) smoked bacon, diced
1 large onion, sliced
150 ml/¼ pint/⅔ cup milk
1 litre/1¾ pints/4¼ cups chicken stock (see page 9)
salt and freshly ground black pepper
150 ml/¼ pint/⅔ cup single (light) cream
freshly chopped parsley to garnish

Cook the potatoes in the melted butter in a large saucepan with the bacon and onion for 10 minutes, or until tender.

Add the milk and stock, season and simmer for 1 hour.

Blend half of the soup in a food processor and return to the pan with the remaining soup. Stir in the cream and heat through, but do not allow the soup to boil.

Garnish with parsley and serve immediately.

CHICKEN BISQUE

Serves 6

15 g/¹/₂ oz/1 tablespoon butter
1 carrot, diced
1 onion, diced
1 celery stick, chopped
1 bouquet garni
450 g/1 lb cooked chicken meat, shredded
150 ml/¹/₄ pint/²/₃ cup dry white wine
2 tablespoons brandy
1.15 litres/2 pints/5 cups basic chicken stock (see page 9)
2 tablespoons short-grain rice
salt and freshly ground black pepper
2 tablespoons sherry
3 tablespoons double (thick) cream

Melt the butter in a large saucepan. Add the vegetables and bouquet garni, cover and simmer for 7 minutes or until softened. Add the chicken, wine and brandy and boil for 2 minutes to reduce the liquid.

Add 250 ml/8 fl oz/1 cup the of stock and simmer for 5 minutes. Add the remaining stock, rice and seasoning. Cover and simmer for 20 minutes, or until the rice is cooked.

Remove the bouquet garni and place the soup in a food processor. Blend until smooth and then press through a sieve.

Return the soup to the pan and heat through. Add the sherry and cream and simmer for 2 minutes, but do not boil. Serve immediately.

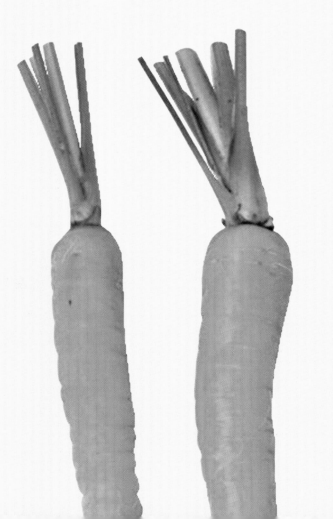
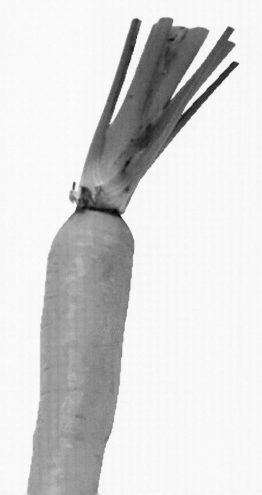

CHICKEN AND OKRA GUMBO

Serves 4

1.5 kg/3¹/₄ lb chicken
salt
1 teaspoon cayenne pepper
1 teaspoon ground black pepper
450 g/1 lb okra, thinly sliced
1 onion, chopped
2 tomatoes, peeled and chopped
1 green (bell) pepper, seeded and chopped
475 ml/16 fl oz/2 cups basic chicken stock (see page 9)
1 tablespoon roux
4 spring onions (scallions), chopped
2 tablespoons freshly chopped parsley

Cut the chicken into portions and reserve any fat from the neck and back. Sprinkle with a little salt and the cayenne and black pepper. Heat the reserved fat in a covered saucepan and add the chicken. Turn to brown on all sides, remove the chicken and reserve.

Add the okra, onion, tomatoes and green pepper to the pan. Pour in the chicken stock, cover and cook over a medium heat for about 40 minutes or until the okra is tender.

Uncover the saucepan and add the roux. Cook for another 30 minutes, then add the chicken. Cook for 45–60 minutes until the chicken is tender and cooked through.

Stir in the spring onions and parsley, adjust the seasoning and cook for 5 minutes. Serve the gumbo ladled over cooked rice or with rice as an accompaniment.

SEAFOOD GUMBO

Serves 4

1 teaspoon salt
1 teaspoon cayenne pepper
1 teaspoon freshly ground black pepper
225 g/8 oz okra, sliced
3–4 tablespoons olive oil
few drops of white vinegar
1 garlic clove, crushed
250 ml/8 fl oz/1 cup basic fish stock (see page 9)
1 large tomato, chopped
2 onions, finely chopped
2 medium-sized crabs
450 g/1 lb prawns (shrimp), heads removed
1 red (bell) pepper, seeded and chopped
6 tablespoons roux
3 spring onions (scallions), chopped

In a small bowl, mix the salt and peppers and reserve. Place the okra, oil, vinegar, garlic, stock, tomato and quarter of the onion in a large saucepan with 1 teaspoon of the salt and pepper mixture. Cook, covered, over a medium heat for 1 hour, stirring frequently.

Meanwhile, half fill a large saucepan with water and add the crabs, cover and cook for 4 minutes. Remove and allow to cool. Peel and de-vein the prawns and place the shells in the saucepan. Remove the claws from the crab and place in the saucepan. Add 2.5 litres/ 4¹/₂ pints/2³/₄ quarts of water and bring to the boil. Boil slowly for 1 hour. Remove from the heat and drain, reserving the liquid. Return the liquid to a clean saucepan.

Add the remaining onion, the red pepper, cooked okra, salt and pepper mixture and the roux. Bring to the boil, stirring, then reduce the heat and simmer for 1 hour.

Meanwhile, scrape any crabmeat from the shells and add to the gumbo. Continue to cook for 45 minutes over a medium heat. Add the prawns and cook for 5 minutes more until they turn pink. Stir in the spring onions and serve over cooked rice.

CHICKEN AND SALAMI GUMBO

Serves 4

¹/₂ teaspoon salt
1 teaspoon cayenne pepper
1 teaspoon freshly ground black pepper
1 kg/2¹/₄ lb chicken
250 ml/8 fl oz/1 cup roux
1 onion, chopped
1 green (bell) pepper, seeded and chopped
1 celery stick
2.5 litres/4¹/₂ pints/2³/₄ quarts basic chicken stock
 (see page 9)
450 g/1 lb salami, chopped
few drops of Tabasco sauce
freshly chopped parsley to garnish

Mix the salt and peppers together in a small bowl. Remove the fat from the neck and back of the chicken and reserve. Cut the chicken into small pieces. Sprinkle half of the salt and pepper mixture over the chicken. Heat the reserved fat in a covered saucepan and cook the chicken until browned all over. Remove the chicken and reserve.

Warm the roux over a low heat and add the onion, green pepper, celery and stock. Add the remaining salt and pepper mixture and bring to the boil. Reduce the heat and cook for 1 hour.

Add the chicken and simmer for 1–1¹/₄ hours until tender. Remove from the heat and allow to stand for 10 minutes. Skim off any surface fat and add the Tabasco sauce and parsley. Serve ladled over cooked rice.

SWEETCORN AND CRAB BISQUE

Serves 4

1 tablespoon butter
1 tablespoon plain (all-purpose) flour
1.8 litres/3 pints/2 quarts basic fish stock (see page 9)
475 ml/16 fl oz/1 cup double (heavy) cream
400 g/14 oz can sweetcorn, drained
1/2 teaspoon cayenne pepper
1 teaspoon dried basil
1 teaspoon dried marjoram
225 g/8 oz canned white crabmeat, drained
3 spring onions (scallions), chopped

Melt the butter in a large saucepan and add the flour, stirring to make a roux. Cook for 1 minute. Stir in the stock and half of the cream, the sweetcorn, seasoning and herbs. Simmer for 25 minutes.

Stir in the crabmeat and simmer for 3–4 minutes longer. Stir in the remaining cream and the spring onions and serve.

OYSTER AND ASPARAGUS SOUP

Serves 4

900 ml/1½ pints/3¾ cups basic fish stock (see page 9)
225 g/8 oz asparagus spears (stalks), chopped
400 ml/14 fl oz/1¾ cups heavy (double) cream
1 teaspoon dried thyme
1 teaspoon dried basil
large pinch of salt
large pinch of ground black pepper
large pinch of cayenne pepper
12 oysters, shucked
freshly chopped parsley to garnish

Heat the stock in a large saucepan and cook the asparagus for 3–4 minutes. Remove from the stock and reserve.

Add the cream and bring to the boil over a high heat. Stir in the herbs, salt and pepper and simmer slowly, whisking frequently, for about 30 minutes.

Add the oysters and asparagus to the soup and stir in the parsley. Cook for 4–5 minutes and serve immediately.

DUCK AND SAUSAGE GUMBO

<u>Serves 4</u>

1 tablespoon salt
2 teaspoons cayenne pepper
2 teaspoons ground black pepper
1 x 1.5 kg/3¼ lb duck, cut into servings
60 g/2 oz/½ cup plain (all-purpose) flour
125 ml/4 fl oz/½ cup olive oil
2.5 litres/4½ pints/2¾ quarts basic chicken stock
(see page 9)
1 onion, chopped
1 yellow (bell) pepper, seeded and chopped
1 celery stick, chopped
250 ml/8 fl oz/1 cup roux
225 g/8 oz smoked sausage, chopped
freshly chopped parsley to garnish

Mix the salt and peppers and set aside. Place the duck pieces in a large bowl and sprinkle over a third of the salt and pepper mix.

Place the flour in a saucepan and add the remaining salt and pepper mixture. Turn the duck in the seasoned flour to coat well.

Heat the oil in a large frying pan (skillet) and cook the duck until browned on all sides. Remove from the pan and reserve.

Place the stock in a large saucepan with the onions, yellow pepper, celery and roux. Bring to the boil, reduce the heat and simmer for 1 hour.

Add the duck to the pan with the sausage and simmer for 1 hour or until the duck is cooked and tender. Remove from the heat and allow to stand for 10 minutes. Skim the fat from the surface and stir in the parsley. Serve ladled over cooked rice.

MIXED FISH AND BACON CHOWDER

Serves 4

225 g/8 oz white and smoked fish fillets, such as cod
or haddock, mixed
2 leeks, sliced
225 g/8 oz potatoes, diced
125 g/4 oz/¹/₂ cup canned tomatoes
30 g/1 oz/¹/₄ cup smoked streaky bacon, chopped
600 ml/1 pint/2¹/₂ cups basic fish stock (see page 9)
2 teaspoons freshly chopped oregano
salt and freshly ground black pepper
200 ml/7 fl oz/³/₄ cup milk
60 g/2 oz/¹/₄ cup frozen sweetcorn
1 tablespoon butter
90 g/3 oz/³/₄ cup Cheddar cheese, grated
cayenne pepper to garnish

Prepare the fish, leeks and potatoes and set
aside. Sieve the tomatoes. Place the bacon in
a large saucepan and heat gently to release
the fat. Add the leeks to the pan and sauté
for 5 minutes, then stir in the potato and
sieved tomatoes.

Add the fish stock and oregano and bring to
the boil, stirring. Season well and simmer for
15 minutes until the potatoes are tender.

Stir in the fish and sweetcorn, cover and
simmer for 10 minutes until the fish is cooked.
Stir in the butter and remove from the heat.

Sprinkle with cheese and serve garnished with
cayenne pepper.

ncluded in this chapter are the real hearty soups which warm us in winter and only need fresh bread or rolls as an accompaniment to make a filling meal. Packed with goodness, the soups are thickened with pulses, lentils, rice and pasta for really tasty dishes.

CABBAGE SOUP WITH CHEESE DUMPLINGS

Serves 6

60 g/2 oz/¹/₄ cup butter

2 small leeks, finely chopped

¹/₂ green cabbage, finely chopped

250 g/9 oz meaty bacon bones

1 tablespoon plain (all-purpose) flour

2 litres/3¹/₂ pints/2¹/₄ quarts basic chicken stock
 (see page 9)

1 teaspoon salt

freshly ground black pepper

¹/₂ teaspoon caraway seeds

1 tablespoon white vinegar

For the dumplings

90 g/3 oz/³/₄ cup self raising flour

90 g/3 oz/³/₄ cup mature (sharp) Cheddar cheese,
 finely grated

1 egg, beaten

1 tablespoon milk, optional

1 tablespoon freshly chopped parsley

salt and freshly ground black pepper

chopped parsley to garnish

Melt the butter in a large saucepan, add the leeks and sauté over a low heat for 5 minutes. Add the cabbage, bacon bones and flour and stir well. Pour in the chicken stock, salt, pepper, caraway seeds and vinegar. Bring to the boil, reduce the heat and simmer for 1 hour.

Meanwhile, place all the dumpling ingredients in a mixing bowl and mix together well to make a firm dough. Divide the dough into 18 equal pieces and with wet hands, roll into walnut-sized balls. Leave to stand until required.

Remove the bacon bones from the soup and cut away any meat. Return the meat to the soup, adjust the seasoning to taste and add extra stock if required. Bring the soup back to the boil and add the dumplings, one at a time. Reduce the heat and simmer for 10 minutes, or until the dumplings have doubled in size. Ladle into soup bowls and serve, garnished with parsley.

MINESTRONE

Serves 8

225 g/8 oz/1¹/₄ cups dried haricot or kidney beans
225 g/8 oz/1¹/₂ cups salt pork, diced
2 garlic cloves, finely chopped
1 Spanish onion, quartered
2.25 litres/4¹/₂ pints/2³/₄ quarts basic chicken stock (see page 9)
4 carrots, finely sliced
4 celery stalks, finely sliced
¹/₂ small green cabbage, sliced
4 large ripe tomatoes, chopped
225 g/8 oz green beans, cut into 2.5 cm/1 inch lengths
225 g/8 oz green peas, shelled
300 g/11 oz macaroni, broken into 5 cm/2 inch lengths
¹/₂ teaspoon freshly ground black pepper
salt
2 tablespoons freshly chopped parsley
2 tablespoons olive oil
4 tablespoons grated Parmesan cheese

Soak the dried beans overnight in cold water. Drain and place in a large pan of unsalted water. Bring to the boil and boil rapidly for 10 minutes, reduce the heat and simmer until the beans are just tender.

Sauté the pork in a frying pan (skillet) until golden, add the garlic and onion and cook until just soft. Transfer the mixture to a large saucepan and add the stock and remaining vegetables, except the peas. Bring to the boil, reduce the heat and simmer gently for 1 hour.

Twenty minutes before serving, add the peas and macaroni to the soup. Return to the boil and cook until the macaroni is tender. Add a little extra water to the soup if required, season with salt and pepper and add the parsley and oil.

Serve immediately, sprinkled with the grated Parmesan cheese.

SPICY RICE SOUP

Serves 4-6

60 g/2oz/¹/₄ cup butter
2 onions, chopped
1 tablespoon garam masala
225 g/8 oz/1¹/₄ cup long-grain rice
1.15 litres/2 pints/5 cups basic chicken stock (see page 9)
1 teaspoon turmeric
grated rind of 1 lemon
125 ml/4 fl oz/¹/₂ cup coconut milk

Melt the butter in a large saucepan and sauté the onions until softened. Add the garam masala and stir for 2 minutes. Stir in the rice to coat the grains and pour in the stock. Add the turmeric and bring to the boil. Stir, cover and cook over a very low heat for 20 minutes until the rice is cooked.

Add the lemon rind and coconut milk and cook for a few minutes. Ladle into soup bowls and serve.

BARLEY SOUP WITH PARSLEY

Serves 6-8

90 g/3 oz/$^{1}/_{2}$ cup split peas
2 onions, chopped
a bouquet garni
175 g/6 oz/1 cup barley
a piece of lamb neck fillet, trimmed of fat
2.25 litre/3$^{3}/_{4}$ pints/2$^{1}/_{2}$ quarts water
salt and freshly ground black pepper
3 carrots, chopped
1 swede (rutabaga), chopped
3 parsnips, chopped
30 g/1 oz/$^{1}/_{2}$ cup parsley, chopped
3 tablespoons freshly chopped parsley

Put the split peas in a bowl and pour boiling water over them to cover. Leave to stand for 1 hour to soften. Drain.

In a large saucepan, place the peas, onions, bouquet garni, barley, lamb, water, salt and pepper. Bring to the boil and cover, then reduce the heat and simmer for 1 hour.

Add the carrots, swede, parsnips and 30 g/1 oz/$^{1}/_{2}$ cup of the parsley. Simmer for 45–60 minutes until all the vegetables are soft.

Serve ladled into soup bowls with the extra parsley sprinkled on top.

CORIANDER (CILANTRO) AND RICE SOUP

Serves 4

1 tablespoon oil

1 tablespoon chopped spring onions (scallions)

1 teaspoon finely chopped root ginger

1 teaspoon ground coriander seeds

1 teaspoon ground cumin seeds

1.5 litres/2¾ pints/7 cups basic chicken stock (see page 9)

juice of half a lemon

1 red chilli

salt and freshly ground black pepper

150 g/5 oz/¾ cup long-grain rice, washed

1 tablespoon plain (all-purpose) flour

250 ml/8 fl oz/1 cup natural yogurt

3 tablespoons coriander (cilantro) leaves

Heat the oil in a large saucepan and add the spring onions, ginger, coriander and cumin. Stir for a few minutes and add the stock, lemon juice, chilli, salt and pepper.

Bring the mixture to the boil and add the rice. Cover the pan, reduce the heat and simmer for 20 minutes.

When the rice is cooked, mix the flour and yogurt together and gradually add to the soup. Do not allow to boil; just cook the soup gently and it will begin to thicken. Stir for 5 minutes and serve with coriander leaves sprinkled on top.

MIXED VEGETABLE SOUP WITH LEEKS

Serves 6-8

2 tablespoons butter
1 Spanish (red) onion, chopped
450 g/1 lb pumpkin, cubed
1 cup cubed potatoes
125 g/4 oz/$^1/_2$ cup shelled broad (fava) beans
500 ml/17 fl oz/2$^1/_4$ cups milk
salt
large pinch of cayenne pepper
1 small leek, finely sliced
500 ml/17 fl oz/2$^1/_4$ cups basic chicken stock (see page 9)
100 g/3$^1/_2$ oz/1$^1/_2$ cups boiled rice
125 ml/4 fl oz/$^1/_2$ cup single (light) cream
2 tablespoons freshly chopped parsley

In a large saucepan, melt half of the butter and sauté the onion until tender. Add the pumpkin, potatoes, beans and milk and bring to the boil. Reduce the heat and simmer for 45 minutes, stirring occasionally so that the vegetables do not stick to the base of the pan.

Transfer the mixture to a food processor in batches and blend to a purée. Return the purée to a clean pan and season with salt and cayenne pepper.

In a small frying pan (skillet), melt the remaining butter and sauté the leek. Add to the vegetable purée with the chicken stock and bring to the boil. Simmer for 10 minutes, then stir in the boiled rice, cream and chopped parsley. Serve immediately.

BROCCOLI POTTAGE

Serves 4-6

60 g/2 oz/¹/₄ cup butter
750 g/1³/₄ lb broccoli, cut into florets with a little stem
 attached
500 ml/17 fl oz/2¹/₄ cups basic chicken stock (see page 9)
¹/₂ teaspoon ground nutmeg
salt and freshly ground black pepper
125 ml/4 fl oz/¹/₂ cup single (light) cream or
 double (heavy) cream
toasted flaked almonds to garnish

Melt the butter in a large saucepan, add the broccoli and cook, stirring regularly, over a medium heat for 10 minutes. Add the stock and seasonings and simmer for 20 minutes or until the broccoli is tender. Remove a few of the cooked florets and reserve as a garnish.

Empty the saucepan into a colander (perforated strainer) over a bowl. Ladle some of the broccoli and stock into a food processor or blender and blend to give a textured purée.

Return the purée to the clean saucepan and repeat with the remaining mixture until all the soup is puréed.

Stir in the cream and reheat over a gentle heat, stirring constantly and without boiling. Serve garnished with toasted almonds and reserved broccoli florets.

ROAST PUMPKIN SOUP WITH SAFFRON THREADS

Serves 4

1.5 kg/3¼ lb whole pumpkin
500 ml/17 fl oz/2¼ cups basic chicken stock (see page 9)
125 ml/4 fl oz/½ cup single (light) cream
125 ml/4 fl oz/½ cup milk
1 teaspoon brown sugar
1–2 teaspoons lemon juice
salt and freshly ground black pepper
a few saffron threads to garnish

Place the whole pumpkin on a baking sheet and cook in a preheated oven at 200°C/400°F/Gas 6 for 1 hour, or until tender when pierced with a fork. Allow to cool for 30 minutes.

Cut the pumpkin in half from top to bottom with a sharp knife and remove and discard the seeds. Scoop the pulp from the shell and place it in a food processor or blender and blend until smooth.

Add the stock, cream, milk, sugar and lemon juice and blend again until well combined.

Pour the purée into a large saucepan and reheat gently without boiling. Season to taste and ladle into soup bowls. Sprinkle with saffron threads and serve.

SPLIT PEA SOUP

<u>Serves 4</u>

275 g/10 oz/1¹/₂ cups split peas, washed
1.25 litres/2¹/₂ pints/5³/₄ cups basic chicken stock
 (see page 9)
1 onion, chopped
15 whole cloves, tied in muslin (cheesecloth) bag
2 teaspoons freshly ground black pepper
1 teaspoon salt
2 teaspoons freshly chopped parsley
1 tablespoon lemon juice

Wash the split peas and soak in water overnight. The next morning, put the peas, stock and onion in a large saucepan and bring to the boil. Remove any scum from the surface.

Add the cloves, pepper and salt. Cover and simmer for 1¹/₄ hours, or until the peas are soft and disintegrating. Remove the muslin bag and squeeze the juices back into the saucepan.

Transfer the soup to a food processor and blend until smooth if required. Alternatively, leave the soup textured. Sprinkle with parsley before serving.

LENTIL SOUP

Serves 6-8

350 g/12 oz/2 cups lentils
2 onions, chopped
3 bacon rashers (slices), chopped
175 g/6 oz/1¹/₂ cups carrots, chopped
1 tablespoon oil
2 litres/3¹/₂ pints/2¹/₄ quarts basic chicken stock
 (see page 9)
1 teaspoon salt
2 teaspoons ground black pepper
1 tablespoon ground coriander
1 teaspoon ground cumin
3 tablespoons freshly chopped mint

Wash the lentils thoroughly and soak in cold water for several hours. Fry the onion and bacon in the oil until the onion is translucent, using a large pan.

Add the drained lentils and carrots, stirring for 1 minute, and then pour the stock into the pan. Season with salt and pepper, coriander and cumin. Bring to the boil and simmer gently until the lentils are cooked.

Garnish with mint and serve.

OLD-FASHIONED SPLIT PEA SOUP

Serves 8

375 g/13 oz/2 cups split peas
2 litres/3¹/₂ pints/2¹/₄ quarts boiling water
450 g/1 lb ham hock
1 large brown onion, chopped
1 medium-sized carrot, chopped
¹/₂ teaspoon freshly ground black pepper
salt

Wash the split peas and soak in water overnight. The next morning, put the peas in a large saucepan with the boiling water. Add the ham, onion, carrot and pepper, cover and simmer for 1–1¹/₂ hours, or until the vegetables are very soft.

Remove the ham, dice the meat and return to the pan, discarding the bone.

Skim off any excess fat and season to taste. Serve with toasted croûtons (see page 147).

SPLIT PEA AND CUMIN SOUP

Serves 4

450 g/1 lb split peas
1 litre/1³/₄ pints/4¹/₄ cups water
1 large brown onion, chopped
2 teaspoons olive oil
2 teaspoons ground coriander
2 teaspoons ground cumin
1 medium-sized carrot, chopped
450 g/1 lb pumpkin, peeled, seeded and chopped
125 g/4 oz/1¹/₂ cups cauliflower, chopped
1 litre/1³/₄ pints/4¹/₄ cups basic vegetable stock
 (see page 10)
freshly ground black pepper
1 tablespoon light soy sauce
freshly chopped parsley to garnish

Wash the split peas and soak in water overnight. The next morning, put the peas in a large saucepan with the water. Bring to the boil uncovered and skim any foam off the top. Cover and cook over a medium heat for 10 minutes, then drain.

In a medium-sized saucepan, cook the onion in the oil for 2 minutes, add the coriander and cumin and continue to cook for 2 minutes more, stirring constantly.

Add the chopped vegetables and stock and bring the mixture to the boil, stirring occasionally.

Reduce the heat and simmer, covered, for 30 minutes. Season with pepper and soy sauce and serve hot, sprinkled with chopped parsley.

EGG AND LEMON SOUP

<u>Serves 6</u>

2 litres/3¹/₂ pints2¹/₄ quarts basic fish stock (see page 9)
90 g/3 oz/¹/₃ cup long-grain rice
3 egg yolks
juice of 2 lemons
salt and freshly ground black pepper

In a large saucepan, bring the stock to the boil and add the rice. Stir the lemon juice and 1 tablespoon cold water into the egg yolks and whisk until frothy.

Add a ladleful of hot stock slowly to the egg and lemon, whisking all the time. Add a second and then a third ladleful of the stock, then pour it back into the saucepan and stir well, off the heat.

Season with salt and pepper to taste. Do not let the soup boil after the egg and lemon juice have been added or it will curdle.

Variation

If you want a creamy soup, leave out the rice and thicken the soup with a little flour, mixed to a paste with cold water. Do this before mixing the stock with the egg and lemon juice.

CHICKEN SOUP

Serves 6

30 g/1 oz/2 tablespoons butter
1 onion, chopped
3 carrots, cut into dice
2 turnips, cut into dice
2 celery sticks, cut into dice
1.8 litres/3 pints/2 quarts, basic chicken stock (see page 9)
90 g/3 oz/$1/2$ cup pearl barley, soaked overnight
2 chicken breasts, cut into bite-sized pieces
1 teaspoon salt
1 teaspoon freshly ground black pepper
2 tablespoons freshly chopped parsley

Melt the butter in a large saucepan and add the onion. Cook over a moderate heat until it turns translucent and then add the other vegetables. Stir for 5 minutes, then add the stock and barley. Cover and simmer for 20 minutes.

Add the chicken meat to the pan and season with salt and pepper. Cover and simmer for 10–15 minutes, or until the vegetables and chicken are cooked.

Ladle into soup bowls and garnish with parsley. Serve.

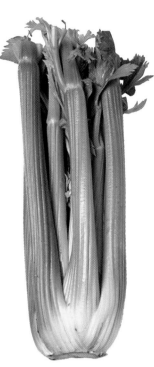

RED LENTIL SOUP

Serves 6

3 tablespoons oil
1 large onion, chopped
1 celery stick with leaves, chopped
375 g/13 oz/2¼ cups red lentils, washed
2 litres/3½ pints/2¼ quarts basic chicken stock
 (see page 9)
salt and freshly ground black pepper
juice of ½ lemon
1 teaspoon ground cumin
garlic croûtons (see page 147) to garnish

Heat the oil in a large saucepan, add the onion and celery and sauté for 6 minutes until the onion softens.

Add the lentils and stock and bring to the boil. Skim away any froth. Reduce the heat and simmer for 30–45 minutes until the lentils have cooked.

If the lentils have not disintegrated, transfer the soup to a food processor and blend to a purée. Return to a clean saucepan and bring to the boil again, adding a little water if a thinner soup is preferred.

Season with salt and pepper, lemon juice and cumin, simmer for 5 minutes more and serve with garlic croûtons.

MINESTRONE GENOVESE WITH PISTOU

Serves 8-10

1 litre/1³/4 pints/4¹/4 cups basic chicken stock (see page 9)

400 g/14 oz can peeled tomatoes, chopped

500 ml/17 fl oz/2¹/4 cups dry white wine

2 onions, diced

3 carrots, diced

1 turnip, diced

2 celery sticks, sliced

2 red (bell) peppers, seeded and diced

1 large courgette (zucchini), sliced

125 g/4 oz/1 cup elbow macaroni or penne pasta

450 g/1 lb can red kidney beans, drained

¹/2 teaspoon turmeric

salt and freshly ground black pepper

Parmesan cheese shavings to garnish

Pistou

1 bunch basil

3 garlic cloves, crushed

60 g/2 oz/¹/2 cup Parmesan cheese, finely grated

4 tablespoons olive oil

salt and freshly ground black pepper

Place the stock in a large saucepan with the tomatoes, wine, onions, carrots, turnip, celery and peppers. Bring to the boil, reduce the heat and simmer for 20 minutes.

Add the remaining soup ingredients, and simmer for another 40 minutes, stirring regularly until all of the vegetables are tender.

Place the basil, garlic and Parmesan in a food processor and blend until finely chopped. With the processor running, slowly add the olive oil through the top of the machine, until a paste is formed. Season to taste.

Serve in large soup bowls with 1 tablespoon of the pistou stirred into each one.

RISI e BISI

Serves 4

30 g/1 oz/2 tablespoons butter
1 lean bacon rasher (slice), rind removed
1 small onion, grated
250 g/9 oz/1¼ cups shelled fresh or frozen peas
1 litre/1¾ pints/4¼ cups basic chicken stock (see page 9)
300 g/11 oz/1¾ cups short-grain rice
60 g/2 oz/½ cup Parmesan cheese, finely grated
salt and freshly ground black pepper
freshly chopped parsley to garnish

Melt the butter in a large saucepan. Add the bacon and onion and sauté over a low heat for 5 minutes, or until the onion is lightly coloured but not browned.

Add the peas and a few tablespoons of the stock. Cover and simmer for 20 minutes for fresh peas and 10–15 for frozen.

Add the rice and half of the remaining stock and bring back to the boil. Reduce the heat, cover and simmer for 15 minutes until the rice is tender.

Add the Parmesan cheese and season with salt and pepper to taste. Add more stock if desired, but the soup should be fairly thick. Sprinkle the parsley over the top, remove from the heat and allow to stand for 1 minute before serving.

LAMB SHANK BROTH

Serves 8

30 g/1 oz/2 tablespoons butter
1 large onion, sliced
4 lamb shanks
3 litres/5¼ pints/3½ quarts water
90 g/3 oz/½ cup barley
3 celery sticks, sliced
2 large carrots, sliced
2 large parsnips, diced
1 teaspoon salt
freshly ground black pepper
freshly chopped parsley to garnish

Melt the butter in a large saucepan. Add the onion and cook over a low heat for 10 minutes. Add the lamb shanks, water, barley, celery, carrots and parsnips. Season with salt and pepper.

Cover and simmer for 1–1¼ hours. Remove the lamb shanks and chop the meat. Return the meat to the pan and discard the bones. Adjust the seasoning to taste.

Serve sprinkled with chopped parsley.

COUNTRY GARDEN VEGETABLE

Serves 10-12

1 large soup bone with meat
450 g/1 lb chuck steak, cut into 5 cm/2 inch cubes
2 tablespoons oil
2 litres/3^1/$_2$ pints/2^1/$_4$ quarts water
1 bay leaf
4 black peppercorns
45 g/1^1/$_2$ oz/^{1}/$_3$ cup pearl barley
1 medium-sized brown onion, chopped
120 g/4 oz mixed vegetables (such as carrots, celery,
 peas or corn)
225 g/8 oz ripe tomatoes, chopped
^{1}/$_2$ teaspoon each freshly chopped rosemary, thyme
 and marjoram
^{1}/$_2$ teaspoon salt
freshly ground black pepper

In a large saucepan, brown the soup bone and chuck steak in the oil over a medium heat, stirring gently.

Add the water, bay leaf and peppercorns, then reduce the heat, cover and simmer for 2 hours.

Remove the bone from the soup, skim any fat from the liquid and add the barley. Simmer for another 45 minutes.

Add the vegetables and herbs and simmer, covered, for 25 minutes, or until the vegetables are tender. Season and remove the bay leaf.

Ladle into soup bowls and serve.

MULLIGATAWNY SIMMER

Serves 8

60 g/2 oz/¹/₄ cup butter
2 onions, finely chopped
2 teaspoons curry powder
2 celery sticks, chopped
2 red eating apples, cored and thinly sliced
1 small turnip, chopped
2 tablespoons plain (all-purpose) flour
1.4 litres/2¹/₂ pints/6¹/₄ cups water
1 tablespoon lemon juice
125 g/4 oz/³/₄ cup long-grain rice
4 small courgettes (zucchini), thinly sliced
salt and freshly ground black pepper
250 ml/8 fl oz/1 cup plain yogurt
3 tablespoons desiccated (shredded) coconut
cooked poppadums (see page 148)

Melt the butter in a large saucepan, add the onions and curry powder and cook slowly for 5 minutes. Add the celery, half of the apples and the turnip. Stir in the flour and cook for 1 minute. Add the water, stirring, and bring to the boil; then reduce the heat and simmer for 20 minutes.

Add the lemon juice and rice. Stir until boiling again and simmer for 15 minutes. Add the remaining apple slices and courgettes and simmer for another 10 minutes, or until they are just tender.

Adjust the seasoning to taste. Mix the yogurt and coconut and serve with the soup, with the poppadums.

ALMOND VELVET

Serves 6

4 leeks, white section only, thinly sliced
60 g/2 oz/^{1}/$_4$ cup butter
1.5 litres/2^3/$_4$ pints/7 cups basic chicken stock (see page 9)
300 g/11 oz/3 cups ground almonds
3 tablespoons short-grain rice
300 ml/^{1}/$_2$ pint/1^1/$_4$ cups single (light) cream
snipped chives or watercress sprigs to garnish

Place the sliced leeks in a colander (perforated strainer) and rinse under cold water. Melt the butter in a large saucepan and cook the leeks over a low heat, stirring frequently, for 15 minutes, or until soft.

Add the stock, ground almonds and rice. Cover and simmer for 30 minutes. Cool slightly and transfer to a food processor. Blend until smooth.

Return the leek purée to the cleaned saucepan and stir in the cream. Reheat the soup until just below boiling. Serve immediately sprinkled with chives or watercress.

This chapter is packed with ideas to finish your soups off in style. Should you want to impress your friends or just your family, the following ideas will quickly turn a simple soup into an elegant and attractive dish. Easy to achieve, it really is worthwhile taking the trouble to garnish your home-made soups.

DEEP-FRIED LEEKS

1 leek, washed
oil for deep-frying

Using a sharp knife, shred the leek very finely lengthways.

Heat the oil for frying in a saucepan or deep-fat fryer to 170°C/340°F and fry the leek for 2–3 minutes until crisp and lightly browned.

Drain well on paper towels and pile into the centre of the soup to serve.

CROÛTONS

4 slices of bread
4 tablespoons olive oil

Remove the crusts from the bread. Brush the bread with olive oil and cut the slices into small cubes.

Heat 2 teaspoons of olive oil in a frying pan (skillet) and add half of the bread cubes. Cook over a low heat, tossing the croûtons until they are golden brown.

Drain on paper towels and repeat with the remaining bread. Serve scattered on top of soup.

FLAVOURINGS FOR CROÛTONS

Garlic – Crush 1 garlic clove into the olive oil before brushing the bread.

Herb – Sprinkle 1 tablespoon freshly chopped or 2 teaspoons dried herbs of your choice into the oil before using to brush the bread.

Seasonings – Use the variety of dried seasonings available in the supermarkets to flavour the croûtons. Stir 1 teaspoon of seasoning into the oil before using to brush the bread.

POPPADUMS

Ready-to-cook poppadums are available in all supermarkets. Either deep-fry in hot oil for 1–2 minutes until golden or buy ready-cooked poppadums. Break into small pieces and use to top soup or serve as an accompaniment.

PASTRY SHAPES

125 g/4 oz prepared puff pastry
milk or beaten egg, for glazing

Heat the oven to 200°C/400°F/Gas 6. Roll the pastry out on a lightly floured surface to 6mm/¼ inch thickness and use cutters to cut out decorative shapes – for example, fish or shells to top fish soup.

Place the pastry shapes on a dampened baking sheet and brush with egg or milk glaze.

Cook in the preheated oven for a few minutes until risen and golden. Serve as a soup topper.

FRIED GINGER

5 cm/2 inch piece root ginger
oil for frying

Use a sharp knife to slice the ginger very thinly.

Heat the oil in a frying pan (skillet) and cook over a medium heat until crisp and browned.

Drain on paper towels and spoon into the centre of the soup before serving.

VEGETABLE CHIPS

1 large potato, peeled
1 medium-sized carrot, peeled
1 cooked beetroot, peeled
oil for deep-frying

Thinly slice the potato, carrot and beetroot and cook in boiling water for 10 minutes. Drain well on paper towels.

Meanwhile, heat the oil for deep-frying in a large saucepan or deep fat fryer to 170°C/340°F.

Fry the sliced, blanched vegetables in the oil for 2–3 minutes until they crispen and turn golden brown. Drain and pat dry on paper towels. Serve with hot soup.

HERBS

Small sprigs of herbs look most attractive as a simple garnish for any soup. Vary the herb to suit the flavour of the soup – for example, basil for tomato soups; thyme or parsley for winter vegetable or meat soups; tarragon for chicken soup.

Freshly chopped fresh herbs are perfect to sprinkle over soup for added flavour just before serving.

CREAMS AND YOGURT

Double (heavy), single (light) or soured creams and plain yogurt are ideal to swirl into soups before serving or to spoon into the centre to be garnished with fresh herbs.

To swirl cream or yogurt into the soup, spoon a spiral shape gently on to the top of the soup with a teaspoon. To feather the swirl, just drag a cocktail stick (wooden toothpick) gently through the swirl.

FLAVOURED BUTTERS

These are delicious stirred into hot soup just before serving and are ideal for adding extra flavour. To make the butter for four servings, soften 2 tablespoons butter in a dish. Stir in the flavouring of your choice – for example, 1 crushed garlic clove, 2 teaspoons of freshly chopped herbs, 1 finely chopped red chilli pepper, a large pinch of cayenne pepper, 2 teaspoons of tomato purée (paste) or 1 tablespoon of finely grated Parmesan cheese.

Spoon the butter on to a piece of greaseproof (waxed) paper and shape into a small cylinder. Roll in the paper and chill. Slice the butter and float on the soup just before serving.

DUMPLINGS

These are great for popping on top of a soup to make it a really filling dish. Flavour the dumplings as liked, either with 2 tablespoons of freshly chopped herbs, with 90 g/3 oz/ $^3/_4$ cup grated cheese, or with $^1/_2$ teaspoon cayenne pepper or chilli powder. Add 2 teaspoons of toasted sesame or cumin seeds to the mixture or sprinkle over the top just before serving.

Basic Recipe

90 g/3 oz/$^3/_4$ cup self-raising flour
I egg, beaten
I tablespoon milk
salt and freshly ground black pepper

Place all the dumpling ingredients in a mixing bowl with the flavouring of your choice and bring together to make a firm dough.

Take small portions of the dough and, with wet fingers, roll them into walnut-sized balls.

Place the dumplings in the hot soup, 10 minutes before serving, and simmer until the dumplings have doubled in size and are cooked through.

FRUIT AND VEGETABLE SHAPES

Use a melon baller to make small melon or cucumber balls to float on the top of your chilled soups, or small, shaped cutters to cut thinly sliced vegetables or fruits.

Simple small florets of cauliflower or broccoli, or carrot and courgette (zucchini) matchsticks are also a great garnish.

SHREDDING AND SHAVING

Shred herbs or hams and salamis to set in the centre of soups with a foreign flavour, or shred herbs such as basil and vegetables such as spinach as a central garnish.

Citrus fruit zest is ideal, either grated or shredded with a zester, to add colour.

GARLIC BREAD

Serves 4

60 g/2 oz/¹/₄ cup butter
2 garlic cloves, crushed
16 thick slices French stick

Mix the butter and garlic well in a small bowl. Spread the butter on both sides of each slice of bread.

Stand the bread on a sheet of kitchen foil and cook in a pre-heated oven at 190°C/375°F/Gas 5 for 10 minutes until golden brown.